TAKE CARE OF
YOURSELF

SURVIVE AND THRIVE
IN CHRISTIAN MINISTRY

PABLO MARTINEZ
FOREWORD BY LINDSAY BROWN

Lausanne Library

TAKE CARE OF YOURSELF

SURVIVE AND THRIVE
IN CHRISTIAN MINISTRY

PABLO MARTINEZ

FOREWORD BY LINDSAY BROWN

Take Care of Yourself: Survive and Thrive in Christian Ministry

Hendrickson Publishers Marketing, LLC
P. O. Box 3473
Peabody, Massachusetts 01961-3473

ISBN 978-1-68307-178-5

All Scripture quotations, unless otherwise indicated, are taken from the Holy Bible, New International Version®, NIV®. Copyright © 1973, 1978, 1984, 2011 by Biblica, Inc.™ Used by permission of Zondervan. All rights reserved worldwide. www.zondervan.com. The 'NIV' and 'New International Version' are trademarks registered in the United States Patent and Trademark Office by Biblica, Inc.™

Scripture quotations marked RSV are taken from the Revised Standard Version of the Bible, copyright © 1946, 1952, 1971 by the Division of Christian Education of the National Council of the Churches of Christ in the United States of America. Used by permission. All rights reserved.

Printed in the United States of America

First Printing—June 2018

Cover design by John Ruffin

Contents

Foreword

This little book is a gem. It could be a lifesaver for someone in Christian ministry. I trust it will bring welcome restoration for any who have lost their joy in the heat of the battle, or simply become worn down.

I'm sure it will provide a soothing balm for the honourably wounded. I wish I had read it in my early twenties when I began working in full-time ministry. I was inspired by the biographies of Robert Murray McCheyne, who died aged twenty-nine, Henry Martyn, who died at thirty-one, and Jim Elliot, who was murdered aged twenty-eight. I was influenced by others who said they would rather 'burn out than rust out.' For my first four years in ministry as a young student worker, I thought days off and holidays were for wimps! So I filled my holidays with ministry opportunities in the UK and overseas.

Then something changed—I was given a sabbatical period for nine months and suddenly experienced exhaustion as I stopped the constant whirr of activity. Six people I had mentored became student workers, and also experienced some form of physical breakdown or health problems. It caused

me to realize that I had provided a poor and in-
adequate model, and I needed to re-think it. Later,
I saw that I had a deficient view of God, both as
a Father who lovingly cares for his children and
as a Creator who gives his people all things to be
enjoyed richly and freely.

There must be many Christians in ministry
who behaved like me, adopting a sub-Christian and
indeed rather platonic worldview, where the body
is seen as being unimportant. Pablo Martinez provides a healthy antidote to that. The book is replete
with choice statements and powerful principles,
such as 'a fruitful ministry is not the same as a full
ministry'; 'the problem is not working too much,
but resting (renewing) too little'; 'we are not human
doings but human beings'; and 'we must learn not
only from [Jesus'] doing but also from his stopping.'

As I read this book, I was reminded of the apostle Paul's exhortation to the Ephesian elders at the
end of his last missionary journey. He was on his
way to Jerusalem 'not knowing what will happen
[to him] there.' He sent a messenger to Ephesus, a
full day's journey away, to find the elders and bring
them to Miletus so he could meet with them before
he sailed. The passage is highly charged and very
moving (Acts 20:17–38). The apostle urges the elders to 'keep watch over yourselves and all the flock
of which the Holy Spirit has made you overseers'
(v. 28). Note the vital order of that command. This
book is a perceptive commentary on those critical
first four words.

Pablo Martinez is Spain's leading evangelical psychiatrist. In his mid-twenties, he made a choice which set the direction of his life. He had the opportunity to engage in student ministry or become Spain's first evangelical psychiatrist. He chose the latter and has been the means of blessing, help and deep-seated counsel to thousands. His previous books, *A Thorn in the Flesh* and *Praying with the Grain*, have been sources of great encouragement and help to many hard-pressed believers.

This book provides liberation for those who fail to appreciate the wonder of God's creation and his fatherly care for his children. More than that, it provides a wonderful sense of the wholeness that the Christian gospel brings to those who place their trust in Christ as Saviour, their dependence on God as Father and Creator, and who draw on the sustaining help and support of the Holy Spirit.

The strange paradox is that those who follow Pablo's advice to take care of their bodies and enjoy God's creation will find that their joy in Christ and the gospel is deepened, and their commitment to serve in Christian ministry enhanced.

I am pleased, too, to see the appendix on handling the past. Over the years I have met many students and Christian workers who carry deep burdens from their past. We have waited a long time for a chapter like this, which I'm sure will bring profound help.

For some, this book will be exhilarating, for others, it will be liberating, and for many, it will be an eye-opener. My prayer is that for all readers it will be a source of enrichment and joy.

Lindsay Brown, General Secretary
International Fellowship of Evangelical Students
(IFES) 1991–2007
International Director
Lausanne Movement 2008–2016

Chapter 1

'Jars of Clay'

*'All the unhappiness of men comes from one thing,
which is not knowing how to be at rest in a room.'*

Pascal[1]

*'They made me keeper of the vineyards;
but my own vineyard I have not kept!'*

Song of Songs 1:6b, RSV

Some people never think of others; that is the paradigm of a selfish person. Others, on the other hand, never think of themselves and become the paradigm of a fatigued person with a restless life. Neither of these two ways of living pleases God, even though the latter may sound more 'spiritual.'

When Robert Murray McCheyne, a young Scottish minister, lay dying at the age of twenty-nine, he turned to a friend and said: 'God gave me a message to deliver and a horse to ride. Alas I have killed the horse and now I cannot deliver the message.'

---

1. Blaise Pascal, *Pensees*, ed. Michel Le Guern, Folio classique (Paris: Gallimard, 1977), fragment 126, 118. French original: 'Tout le malheur des hommes vient d'une seule chose, qui est de ne pas savoir demeurer en repos dans une chambre.'

What a graphic picture of spiritual passion turned to overexertion.

Billy Graham was once asked, 'What would you change if you could start your life again?' He replied: 'I would preach only once a day.' The words of this respected man of God echo a profound and most important principle: a fruitful ministry is not the same as a full ministry packed with activities and unceasing action.

After many years of counselling Christian workers about the danger of exhaustion and about its prevention, I have come to a conclusion similar to Billy Graham's: the problem is not working too much, but resting (renewing) too little. The purpose of this book is not to make you work less but to help you rest more and renew yourself better.

We are not human doings but human beings

Many times we neglect the care of our 'vineyard' because we want to deny God's original design for us: he made us human beings, not human doings. Our identity and value before God come primarily from who we are, not from what we do. This divine design includes a balance between working and resting, giving and receiving. If this balance is broken, there is a danger that, like the writer of the Song of Songs, we will neglect our own vineyard while we are caring for the vineyards of others.

Caring for our own life means guarding our physical, emotional and spiritual wellbeing. According to the Bible, this is not only a right but a duty; it is part of good stewardship to care for ourselves. To put it in other words, in the same way that we have a ministry, we also need a 'monastery,' a place and time to rest, to be still and to refresh our whole person. Our public ministry will be greatly enhanced if we learn to spend time in our private 'monastery.'

Caring for Your Own Vineyard: Waste of Time or Wise Investment?

Why is caring for your own vineyard not only a right but a duty? In a *selfist* society where 'feeling good' and 'being happy' are idols worshipped by many people, this might sound like self-centredness.

God has a lot to say on the care of ourselves. We need to regain the divine wisdom on this issue and escape the hedonism that entangles our world today. God created work, but he also created rest. There is indeed a biblical teaching—a theology—on work and leisure.

The biblical description of human beings—biblical anthropology—explains who we are and, particularly, *how* we are—our condition—after the multiple fractures caused by the Fall. From this reality we can outline three reasons why we should take care of ourselves.

- Because it is God's will for us: We were created in his image, so this is related to God's original *design*. God included rest in his creation and he commanded rest. Caring for ourselves is therefore an expression of obedience.

- Because of our fragility: We are jars of clay, not of iron. Caring for ourselves is related to our human *condition*. It is an expression of humility—of dependence on God's grace.

- Because it is part of good stewardship: We are temples of the Holy Spirit, so caring for ourselves is part of our *responsibility* and is an expression of maturity.

In summary, the practice of rest and the care of yourself, far from being a selfish act, is an exercise of godliness and an expression of holiness.

The consequences of not keeping your own vineyard can be harmful, even disastrous. They affect other people besides yourself, especially your loved ones, and also your work (1 Timothy 5:4,8). So neglect of ourselves, far from being a sign of a spiritual attitude, can be a serious mistake and even a sin. Paul urged Timothy to learn this principle when he was still young, in his learning years. His warning 'take care of yourself' (see 1 Timothy 4:16) contains one of the keys in Christian work. Notice the order: first the person has to be all right, and then comes the work (the teaching). If the person is not all right, the quality of the work will be affected. A healthy minister is likely to have a healthy and fruitful ministry.

It is noteworthy that Paul approaches this issue with exquisite balance. His advice to Timothy is immediately preceded by an exhortation to effort and consecration: 'Be diligent in these matters; give yourself wholly to them, so that everyone may see your progress' (4:15). A clear appeal to a consecrated life is followed by an equally clear call to 'take care of yourself' (see v. 16). How much we need the same balance in our lives!

Thank God for leisure times!

It may surprise you, but some Christian workers feel guilty when they rest. They have a mistaken concept of leisure and they wrongly believe that God wants them to be *doing* something all the time (they are 'human doings'!). It is important to remember that leisure and laziness are very different things.[2] Laziness is wrong because it is a waste of time; leisure,[3] on the other hand, can be a wise way to invest your time. In laziness you do nothing; in rest you are actively engaged in renewing yourself, restoring your physical, emotional and spiritual energy. By so doing you are obeying God, renewing your dependency on his grace, and acting as a good steward of your time and your life.

---

2. For a further study on the subject, see Leland Ryken, *Work and Leisure in Christian Perspective* (Leicester: Inter-Varsity Press, 1987).

3. *Leisure*—from the Latin *licere,* to be allowed—is the time at one's disposal, free time, a time that is not under obligation or duty.

'Jars of Clay'

'*But we have this treasure in jars of clay to show
that this all-surpassing power is from God and
not from us.*' (2 Corinthians 4:7)

We are jars of clay, not jars of iron or broken
jars! The Christian worker must be aware of the
glorious nature of the ministry—'that treasure'—
but also of the fragile nature of the minister. We
need to start here, knowing our natural condition.
This will deliver us from making life mistakes, er-
rors that affect our life profoundly. Notice that the
two extremes are equally wrong: we are not jars of
iron, all powerful and never failing individuals; but
God does not want us to be broken jars either. Thus,
we have to be careful with our fantasies of omnipotence, and we should not praise exhaustion per se
as an expression of zeal and commitment.

Fragility has a purpose

What is the benefit of our being 'jars of clay'?
Clay is a fragile material. It gets broken easily. Our
fragility makes us depend fully on the divine supply
of grace and strength every day, 'to show that this
all-surpassing power is from God and not from us'
(2 Corinthians 4:7).

In this sense, our limitations and our fragility
are to our soul what tiredness, hunger and thirst
are to our bodies. They are warning signs that urge
us to seek a daily renewal of God's provision. It is

through our fragility—and not in spite of it—that God fulfils his purposes for our lives and ministries.

Handle with care

We need a clear sense that we are jars of clay if we are to start caring for ourselves. If we don't grasp this, we will not see the need. We must handle a fragile object with care because it is easily broken. It is the same with our lives. Because God made us 'jars of clay,' we are to handle ourselves carefully. I am firmly convinced that our Master does not want his servants to be broken jars. Far from it—God has always intended to protect our fragile vessels from dangers that could spoil them.

As a medical doctor I am fascinated by the Ten Commandments, a superb programme of social, spiritual and personal health. If you study each of the commandments thoroughly, you will discover their unsurpassed preventive (prophylactic) value. Their purpose was to preserve and to promote a good quality of life at all levels. Through the Ten Commandments, God is sending us a clear three-fold message: take care of your relationship with God, take care of relationships with your neighbours, and take care of yourself.

God wants to accomplish his purposes through fragile, even weak servants—jars of clay—but not through burned-out, exhausted servants—broken jars. These broken vessels are in need of prompt repair because the divine design is for us to be healthy and whole, not broken into pieces.

On the other hand, workers who view themselves as iron jars overvalue their capacity and undervalue their limitations. This will lead to problems with boasting and self-sufficiency, the temptation Paul had to face. 'In order to keep me from becoming conceited, I was given a thorn in my flesh' (2 Corinthians 12:6–7). Awareness of our limitations greatly helps us to set limits in our life programme.

We have looked at our condition, what we are like. Let us now consider another clue in the care of ourselves: the sort of life God wants us to live.

'Make It Your Ambition to Lead a Quiet Life'

At first sight, this is a surprising statement. Even more surprising is the context in which Paul places it; namely, the kind of life that pleases God: 'As for other matters, brothers and sisters, we instructed you how to live in order to please God, as in fact you are living. Now we ask you and urge you in the Lord Jesus to do this more and more' (1 Thessalonians 4:1). It sounds like an important appeal. By the end of the section, verse 11, he adds: 'Make it your ambition to lead a quiet life.' Therefore a quiet life is part of holy living. It is not only good for ourselves, but it pleases God.

What is a quiet life? Let Paul himself answer this question on the basis of his own testimony. In his second letter to the Corinthians, the most autobiographical of all the epistles, Paul opens his heart and makes some personal confessions that are very helpful to us.

A quiet life is not a life without problems. 'As servants of God we commend ourselves in every way: in great endurance; in troubles, hardships and distresses; in beatings, imprisonments and riots; in hard work, sleepless nights and hunger . . .' (2 Corinthians 6:4–5). Paul is realistic. Christian ministry is not a holiday experience but tough work! Paul does not hide the cost of discipleship. Our salvation is free, but there are no bargains in discipleship. Following Christ has a cost.

A quiet life is not a life without stress. 'Besides everything else, I face daily the pressure of my concern for all the churches' (2 Corinthians 11:28). Pressure and concern could be also rendered as worry and anxiety. The modern word that best defines this pair of emotions is stress. The conclusion is clear: troubles and stress are inevitable for any Christian worker who takes their calling seriously.[4] There is no blessing without sacrifice. Dangers, toils and tribulation are a frequent companion in Christian service.

Our goal as servants of God is not to live a life free of trouble or pressures. This is not a biblical idea and it is not realistic either. The goal is to avoid permanent stress. Occasional stress is like an ally that helps us overcome difficulties and

---

4. For more on this, see experienced missionary psychiatrist Marjory F Foyle, *Honourably Wounded: Stress among Christian Workers* (London: Monarch Books, 2001).

troubles; permanent stress is an enemy that drains our energy and causes dryness in our vineyard. To live under permanent stress cannot be pleasing to God, who established different sorts of rest in his creation (see chapter two). Permanent stress is an enemy to be defeated, a signal that something is going wrong in our life and needs to be corrected.

A quiet life is a life without turbulence. Remarkably, the Greek word rendered as 'lead a quiet life' literally means 'without turbulence.' It conveys the idea of silence (it was used for the quietness of the night), peace, rest and even leisure. It implies being still, exactly the opposite of stress. A quiet life reflects the deep peace and rest that come from God's presence with us.

Exhaustion does not make us more holy. In 2 Corinthians 8 and 9 we discover an important principle on giving (offering) and self-giving: generosity is not measured by the total quantity you give but by your attitude and purpose. The churches in Macedonia 'welled up in rich generosity. . . . Entirely on their own . . . They gave themselves first of all to the Lord, and then by the will of God also to us' (8:2,4,5). Paul is impressed by—and praises—primarily the spirit behind their self-giving.

Great zeal for the Lord does not mean great stress for you!

We tend to believe that the more we give ourselves—quantity of time, energy, etc—the more holy we are. But quantity per se does not make you more spiritual. A generous self-giving ministry does not imply a masochist spirit that leads you to exhaustion. It cannot be God's will for his servants to jeopardize their health or their family life. Generosity in God's service is not at odds with order and balance, two features that God stamped as a seal on his creation and on his creatures. Notice that 'order' (*cosmos*) is one of the hallmarks of God's world. Order and balance, therefore, should be a hallmark of God's servants too.

A quiet life is a life of glorious paradoxes

This quiet life is not incompatible with the cost of discipleship. Paul would never have advised the Thessalonians or Timothy so earnestly on this line if he believed it was utopia. The apostle was a deep thinker, but he also had a practical pastoral heart.

The coexistence of a quiet life with the troubles of Christian ministry is better understood through a passage like 2 Corinthians 4:8–9: 'We are hard pressed on every side, but not crushed; perplexed, but not in despair; persecuted, but not abandoned; struck down, but not destroyed.' Notice this text follows straight after the statement that we are 'jars of clay.' A parallel text is 2 Corinthians 6:9–10: 'Known, yet regarded as unknown; dying, and yet we live on; beaten, and yet not killed; sorrowful, yet always rejoicing; poor, yet making many rich; having nothing, and yet possessing everything.'

These glorious paradoxes reveal to us that the secret of a quiet life does not depend on the absence of problems but on the presence of Christ with us through all these troubles. God's mercy and comfort in Christ make it possible for us to live a quiet life in the midst of any storm. This is what Paul describes in the first chapter: 'Praise be to the God . . . who comforts us in all our troubles, so that we can comfort those in any trouble with the comfort we ourselves receive from God' (2 Corinthians 1:3–4). We cannot avoid the storms in Christian ministry, but we can indeed avoid the turbulence of these storms.

A 'Minor' Issue with Major Consequences

'As dead flies give perfume a bad smell, so a little folly outweighs wisdom and honour.' (Ecclesiastes 10:1)

You may think neglecting your vineyard is a minor issue in your life, or that you have much more important things to do than caring for yourself, so you keep postponing any action related to it. Beware! The small enemy may become the greatest enemy. Small does not mean unimportant.

The wisdom of the Bible warns us that in the same way a bottle of perfume can be spoiled by a dead fly, 'a little folly outweighs wisdom and honour.' Neglecting your vineyard may seem like a 'little folly' to you, but it can bring forth major consequences.

Nature, an endless source of practical lessons, confirms the wisdom of the biblical advice. Did you know that the tiny mosquito is responsible for killing more human beings per year than wars or homicides? A small bug, apparently insignificant, is more dangerous than the fearsome wild beasts. Be careful with the 'mosquitoes' of the Christian life! The devil is a specialist in taking advantage of our weak points. Even when we feel strong, or precisely because we feel strong, we are reminded: 'So, if you think you are standing firm, be careful that you don't fall!' (1 Corinthians 10:12).

Caring for your own vineyard is not a minor issue. Your own life, the wellbeing of your family and the quality of your ministry are at stake. God wants his servants to be good guards of their own vineyards because that is one of the secrets of a fruitful and blessed ministry.

Chapter 2

The Empty Pool Syndrome: When Output Exceeds Input

'But I am weary! I am too weary to be working now, and too tired to sleep . . . I am getting prematurely old, they tell me, and doctors do not give me long to live unless the strain is eased a bit.'

Douglas M Thornton[5]

'Power (energy) has gone out from me.'

Luke 8:46

In all professions you have to give something of yourself. A certain amount of inner energy is always required to perform your work adequately. This is particularly true in the so-called 'caring professions': doctors, nurses, counsellors, social workers. I include here pastors, missionaries and Christian workers because all these professions require direct contact with persons and, particularly, with human needs or pain, whether physical, emotional or spiritual. Such work requires self-giving and, consequently, extra energy.

5. Missionary in Egypt. Quoted by J Oswald Sanders, *Spiritual Leadership* (London: Lakeland Ed, 1967), 109.

One of the healing acts of Jesus illustrates this reality well: 'Someone touched me; I know that power has gone out from me' (Luke 8:46). Among a multitude of people crowding and pressing against him, Jesus clearly perceived that some energy had gone out from him; a needy woman touched the hem of his garment and she was healed. This loss of eneregy was supremely the case with Jesus, but something similar happens to us, as followers of Jesus. Every healing or caring action requires an output of inner energy.

In this sense, as Christian workers we can compare our life to a mountain pool and our energy to water. Two streams of water need to flow at the same time. There is output, water flowing out. This is the emotional and spiritual energy that 'goes out' as we fulfil our calling. Any caring task will bring some expenditure of energy. Being compassionate and empathetic, as Jesus was, implies identification with our neighbour and, therefore, self-giving. You cannot heal or help mechanically, as if you were repairing a car. The essence of caring is love, and loving means self-giving. There are no shortcuts in Christian ministry because we are mainly dealing with people. 'No real lasting good can be done without the outgoing of power and the expenditure of nervous energy.'[6] In ministry there is no such thing as 'zero wear,' or 'total protection' from people's problems.

---

6. Sanders, *Spiritual Leadership*, 109.

For this reason we also need input, water to replenish the pool. This is our personal renewal and refreshment. Whenever there is more output than input, the pool gets emptied little by little, leading finally to what I like to call the 'empty pool syndrome.' We have run out of inner energy. In medicine this condition is called emotional exhaustion or burnout. I prefer to use the illustration of the pool because it reflects more accurately the dynamics of the process, the loss of balance between the two movements, output and input.

The principle of the two movements is seen throughout the natural world. Everything in nature has rhythms which are complementary alternations: winter and summer, night and day. One must follow the other. The book of Ecclesiastes describes this reality with several examples: 'There is a time for everything, and a season for every activity under the heavens: a time to be born and a time to die, a time to plant and a time to uproot . . .' (Ecclesiastes 3:1–8).

The functioning of the heart shows the vital importance of this principle: contraction (diastole) follows expansion (systole). The two movements are successive and complementary. First, the heart receives blood; then it is ready to distribute it. When this rhythm is altered, our life is at risk. Many Christian workers have not learned to be in diastole; their life is a permanent systole. The consequences are harmful for themselves and for those around them.

God uses an illustration similar to the pool in Isaiah 58. He compares his people to a well-watered garden: 'The LORD will guide you always; he will satisfy your needs in a sun-scorched land and will strengthen your frame. You will be like a well-watered garden, like a spring whose waters never fail' (v. 11). Notice the order: first you need to be well-watered (input); then you will naturally become a spring of permanent waters to others (output). What a great motto for the Christian worker! Our prayer should be, 'Lord, make me like a well-watered garden, like a spring whose waters never fail!'

'Stops' with a Purpose

How can we increase our *input* in daily life? Chapters four and five are devoted to the ways God has given us to refill the pool. Here we must note a key practical issue: God established in creation a three-fold rest that we should respect carefully.

- The daily rest: sleep
- The weekly rest: the Sabbath
- The annual rest: a seasonal holiday (nature 'sleeps' in winter)

After many years as a psychiatrist I have not seen a single case of burnout among those who respected this three-fold rest. They are 'stops' with a purpose, the equivalent of the diastole to our heart.

Rest after work is not a human invention, but God's design

The wisdom of the Creator lies behind this design, the same wisdom that made him rest on the seventh day. The Almighty needed no rest, but he wanted to set a model for us. God's rest becomes a paradigm, a compelling pattern to everyone, particularly to his servants. This advice may sound obvious, but many fail here. An astonishing percentage of Christian workers do not respect all three 'stops.' I have dealt with dozens who have not enjoyed an annual break for years!

Sleep is a good investment: 'Watering' your neurons at night

Some people believe that sleeping is a waste of time, a loss of one third of their lives. They cannot be more mistaken! I want to underline the enormous value of sleeping enough for the prevention of exhaustion. Neuroscience has proved recently that while we are sleeping the brain is actively working. It performs an amazing task of refreshment that could be compared to the 'watering of our neurons.' It is a fascinating natural process, and you do not need to be an expert in neurosciences to prove it. When you are tired on a Sunday evening after a busy day, all problems seem big; small issues become giant. The next morning, after a good night's rest, everything looks different!

If God himself rested, we must rest too. In the same way that a 'stop' traffic signal is there for a purpose, God's three-fold rest has a purpose: a healthy and fruitful life. We must beware of our unconscious fantasies of omnipotence!

Oswald Sanders, a hard worker on the verge of exhaustion

The story of Oswald Sanders, a remarkable Christian leader, illustrates the importance of this principle. His book *Spiritual Leadership* has helped thousands of Christian workers, but there is a painful experience behind the book that should not be overlooked. 'He became well known in evangelical circles throughout the world for his efficiency, his skill in reasoning and planning. . . . He was a missionary statesman whose work was firmly grounded in reality.'[7] Considered a master in leadership, his gifts and work were highly admired. He worked hard indeed, but so hard that he nearly suffered burnout. On the verge of exhaustion, he had to learn that resting is a commandment you need to obey, not an option or a luxury.

Notice the admirable balance behind this quotation: 'If the leader is unwilling to pay the price of fatigue for his leadership, it will always be mediocre. . . . If he is wise, however, he will seize every legitimate opportunity for recuperation and

---

7. Timothy Larsen, ed., *Biographical Dictionary of Evangelicals* (Leicester: Inter-Varsity Press, 2003), 576–78.

recreation, or he will limit his own usefulness and ministry.'[8]

We could summarize the practice of the two movements by paraphrasing John Wesley's dictum on money and applying it to our energy: work as much as you can, renew yourself as much as possible and rest as much as you need to.

See When the Pool Is Becoming Empty

'How can I know that my pool is becoming empty?' I am asked this question time and again. It is a crucial point because prevention is always better—and easier—than the cure. As the level of water (our energy) can decrease in a subtle way, we must beware of the warning symptoms before we suffer exhaustion. If we pay attention to them and make the necessary changes (see chapter three), the pool will be refilled.

Moses and Elijah: Giants of the faith who experienced exhaustion

The Bible, with consummate realism, presents us with two of its most illustrious characters experiencing bouts of emotional exhaustion. It is significant that Moses and Elijah, giants of the faith, the symbols of the Law and the Prophets who accompanied Jesus in the Transfiguration, should appear

---

8. Sanders, *Spiritual Leadership*, 109.

as men 'of like nature with ourselves' (James 5:17, RSV). God's providence had a purpose in allowing these episodes of burnout: to leave us 'an example of suffering and patience,' as James explicitly says of Elijah (James 5:10, RSV).

In the case of Moses, the relationship spanning so many years with 'a stiff-necked people' (Deuteronomy 9:6,13), who were disobedient and murmured unceasingly, became a heavy burden for the meek patriarch: 'I cannot carry all these people by myself; the burden is too heavy for me' (Numbers 11:14). A brilliant diagnosis! Overwhelmed by the weight of this responsibility, feeling alone and exhausted, his spirit grew weak. The people's repeated complaining had even drained God's patience. It is not surprising, then, that the patriarch's emotional tension undermined his psychic resistance. One of these crises was so intense that he reached the point of wanting to die (v. 15). Moses was clearly suffering from an empty pool syndrome.

Elijah went through a similar crisis. In 1 Kings 19:1–18 we see a man worn out by the emotional intensity of previous events. The prophet had just experienced one of the peak moments in his life, victory over the prophets of Baal. However, the devil knows well when to attack; hours of great success are one of his favourite targets. Temptation comes mainly in times of great distress or great success. Both extremes make us vulnerable. And now we have the hero of Mount Carmel fleeing like a coward because 'they seek my life, to take it away' (19:10, RSV). How to explain this turnabout? Elijah seems to be another person. The reason is clear: he was exhausted. After a great conflict and then a great victory, he was worn down. He needed to refill the empty pool.

From the experience of these two great men of God, we see warning lights the in four areas explored below. Notice the progressive nature of these symptoms. The order in which they appear reflects the worsening of the process. This is why we should heed the first stages, when there is still time to fill the pool. It is much easier to help someone who is simply discouraged and irritable than someone who wants to die, as was the case with Elijah and Moses.

i. Unusual reactions: Irritability and impatience

'He's hypersensitive, irascible, and everything bothers him. He was not like this before,' the family says. Early signals include irritability, harsh words and little patience with others to the point of causing tension in your relationships. You feel easily hurt or respond to things too quickly and too rudely, especially with those at home. You feel tense, unable to relax as you did before. A change in your character that lasts for more than a few days can be the first warning.

Moses was overcome by anger at Meribah when he struck the rock twice instead of speaking to it, as the Lord had commanded him (Numbers 20:8–13). On another occasion he could not contain his anger against the people's idolatry, breaking into a holy rage as he smashed the tablets of the law into pieces (Exodus 32:19). Remember, this happened to a man who 'was very meek, more than all men that were on the face of the earth' (Numbers 12:3, RSV).

Protest and complaint are common ways of expressing this inner unrest. Anger can show itself in varying ways according to the intensity of the exhaustion, from simple ill-humour to difficulties in self-control like Moses. You tend to blame others, or even God, for a particular situation, complaining that 'they are not treating me well.' Moses 'asked the LORD, "Why have you brought this trouble on your servant? What have I done to displease you that you put the burden of all these people on me? . . . If this is how you are going to treat me, please go ahead and kill me"' (Numbers 11:11,15). Resentment and bitterness may be the final outcome if the condition is not improved.

Isolation—withdrawing from people—is another possible reaction. Elijah 'left his servant there, while he himself went a day's journey into the wilderness' (1 Kings 19:3–4). He preferred to be alone because people felt like a burden. This was also Moses's feeling.

ii. Physical symptoms: Sleep problems and a slower mind

Our body sends early messages warning us that something is wrong. Persistent sleep disturbances, especially insomnia, and a mild decrease of your cognitive (intellectual) abilities are the most common signs. Your brain is working more slowly and you find it difficult to concentrate when reading, writing or preparing a sermon. Eating disorders, either loss of appetite or eating compulsively (weight gain), may be an expression of the inner anxiety.

Notice God's prescription for Elijah's exhaustion: 'The angel of the LORD came back a second time and touched him and said, "Get up and eat, for the journey is too much for you"' (1 Kings 19:7).

iii. Low energy: Fatigue and lack of motivation

'I give up, I can't go on'; 'I feel like a battery that has run out of energy.' A feeling of deep tiredness is a signal that the situation is worsening. It is time for action. Do not postpone taking care of yourself.

This lack of energy can be felt as:

- Loss of interest or motivation over everyday tasks

- Apathy, difficulty in starting any duty

- Everyday work feeling like a burden

- Inability to anticipate things and experience pleasure

- Lack of excitement or enthusiasm about future projects or goals

Nothing seems worth it. A sort of 'Ecclesiastes spirit'—existential boredom—permeates you:

'Everything was meaningless, a chasing after the wind; nothing was gained under the sun' (Ecclesiastes 2:11). In sum, you cannot enjoy your work and ministry anymore. This is the reason why, like Moses and Elijah, you want to give up.

iv. Distorted thoughts: Pessimism and hopelessness

An almost empty pool affects your thoughts. The way you perceive reality is altered and you see everything from a pessimistic and hopeless point of view. These negative thoughts appeared intensely in Moses and Elijah. Both of them evaluated their work harshly and even faltered in their appreciation of God. The Lord patiently corrected their wrong views of reality.

Just as you are overwhelmed by pessimism about your work and about God, you may be overcome by negative thoughts about yourself. The prophet Elijah felt he had been a failure, saying, 'I am no better than my ancestors' (1 Kings 19:4). The less energy you have, the more severely you will judge yourself. This sense of failure usually generates guilt. Unfounded feelings of guilt can be an expression of an incipient depression. All these negative thoughts finally bring forth a loss of hope. The future seems gloomy: *'There's no future left for me.'*

The wrong conclusions caused by distorted thinking could explain why some Christian workers give up their ministry. They believe their reason

to resign is the right one, but they are often unaware of the likely reason behind it: an empty pool
syndrome that was not identified or corrected in
time. If you ever feel like giving up, remember
Moses and Elijah! They were wrong, and God had
to correct their distorted views.

God knows the nature of his servants' problems. He instructed Moses and Elijah to make the
necessary changes and gave them provision to
renew their energy. The result was obvious: Elijah
'got up and ate and drank. Strengthened by that
food, he travelled forty days and forty nights until
he reached Horeb, the mountain of God' (1 Kings
19:8). Shortly afterwards God provided someone
suitable to relieve his burden: the prophet Elisha.
Also, Moses was equipped with a team of helpers
and he went on with renewed strength. Elijah and
Moses were ready to pursue their ministry according to God's *purpose*. Their experience shows us
how the empty pool syndrome, like most crises, is at
the same time a danger and an opportunity. It may
destroy your vocation, but it may also strengthen
it. In the next chapter we will look at mistakes that
lead to exhaustion and how they can help us grow.

In the meantime, check your pool regularly.
Behind every fatigue there is a message we need
to understand. Try to discover what God wants to
tell you through this fatigue. Learn to identify the
'warning lights' in your body and your mind to prevent the empty pool.

Chapter 3

Preventing Mistakes
That Empty the Pool

'All lasting fatigue is a sign that something in our life is not in order, something that needs to be examined before God.'

Paul Tournier[9]

'I wish I had known these things earlier. If I had, I would not have made the mistakes that almost ruined my ministry and my life.' Many Christian leaders come to me with these words. They are aware that their pool was emptied because of wrong concepts, attitudes or practices that needed to be changed.

As we said at the beginning, some stress and weariness in ministry is inevitable. There is a cost of discipleship and leadership that we cannot change, for 'a servant is not greater than his master' (John 15:20). Nevertheless, a good deal of our weariness does not belong to the category of natural Christian weariness, but is the result of mistakes and things that are not in order in our life. This could be called

---

9. *La fatiga en la sociedad contemporánea* (Buenos Aires: La Aurora, 2000), 30.

a '*wrong* weariness.' In this case, we should not say 'the ministry wearied me,' but 'my mistakes in ministry wearied me.' Fatigue, therefore, is not the disease itself, but rather the symptom of a deeper problem. Its treatment is inside us. In other words, if all lasting fatigue is a sign, we need to understand its meaning, the *message* behind it.

There are a variety of mistakes that can lead us to an empty pool condition. Discovering and correcting mistaken judgment in these areas is the purpose of this chapter. I have selected five such incorrect mind-sets that, from my professional experience, seem the most harmful and pervasive.

I. Perfectionism: The Mistake of Trying to Be Flawless

One frequent cause of the empty pool is working under too much pressure. Many times this pressure is not related to any external circumstance but comes from within ourselves. It has to do with our own personality makeup. We tend to put too much pressure upon ourselves. This excessive self-demand is called perfectionism.

What is wrong with perfectionism? Did not Jesus command 'Be perfect, therefore, as your heavenly Father is perfect' (Matthew 5:48)? We need to distinguish between compulsive perfectionism and biblical perfection. The latter is a search for excellence related to spiritual maturity and it seeks to please God. The former arises from insecurity and expresses a need for the approval of others. Understanding their basic differences is an important step towards health and peace.[10]

The word 'perfect' in the New Testament (*teleios*) means 'mature' or 'grown up'. It is in this sense that Paul writes of 'admonishing and teaching everyone with all wisdom, so that we may present everyone fully mature [perfect] in Christ' (Colossians 1:28). Biblical perfection is not a matter of impeccability, but of maturity. Hebrews 5:14 explains this idea: 'But solid food is for the mature [perfect], who by constant use have trained themselves to distinguish good from evil.' Perfection is the maturity that gives us ethical discernment to obey and please God in everything we do. It is God-centred, not people-centred; it has more to do with holy behaviour than with personal achievements.

Compulsive perfectionism, by contrast, is obsessed with results and with making no mistakes. A feeling of dissatisfaction—like you never reach the desired level of achievement—goes alongside all you do. It is like having an inner policeman who keeps saying, 'You could do better. It is not enough.' Compulsive perfectionism leads to compulsive work. Far from being an expression of maturity, it is usually linked to insecurity. Its driving force is not ethical discernment but fear of failure and the need

10. For a further study of this topic I recommend Richard Winter, *Perfecting Ourselves to Death: The Pursuit of Excellence and the Perils of Perfectionism* (Downers Grove, IL: InterVarsity Press, 2005).

to please others. Neither of these are good motivations and, paradoxically, they can be a constraint instead of a stimulus in the Christian ministry.

The best antidote to perfectionism is God's grace. Grasping the soothing balm of grace changes the pressure of perfectionism into the serene conviction that the grace of God reaches where we cannot. This is exactly the message Paul received from God: 'My grace is sufficient for you, for my power is made perfect in weakness' (2 Corinthians 12:9). A full understanding that grace makes us sufficient in all our daily weaknesses can have a revolutionary effect on our ministry. It changed Paul's life altogether.

II. Activism: The Mistake of Trying to Do Too Much

'Better is a handful of quietness than two hands full of toil and a striving after wind.' (Ecclesiastes 4:6, RSV)

Christian leaders are often very gifted people. This is indeed a blessing, but it may become a problem. When you are able to do many things very well and you receive frequent requests from many people, you end up doing too much. Being involved on too many front lines (also known as dispersion) jeopardizes both excellence and health. This is one of the most frequent reasons for failure in ministry. We have to be careful not only with the pressure inside ourselves—that of perfectionism—but also with excessive pressure coming from the outside, forcing us into ever-greater activism.

It is God's will for us to be active, but not hyperactive

Doing too much creates fertile ground for making serious mistakes. How can you know that you are doing too much? There are clear signs: you neglect and eventually harm your health and your relationships, especially with your family. When your health or your loved ones suffer, your life programme needs revision. A crowded diary may make you feel a fulfilled person, but in the long term it makes you a vulnerable person. A 'do not disturb' sign may be necessary at certain times in your life, but a permanent 'do not disturb' indicates that you are trapped in the seductive cage of activism. You need to get out of it as soon as possible.

'Martha, Martha . . . you are worried and upset about many things. . . . Mary has chosen what is better' (Luke 10:41–42). A remarkable description of activism! Martha's problem was 'being upset [literally stressed] about many things.' We should not overlook Jesus' central message here: you may be able to do many things, but very few are really important. A need does not convey an obligation. We cannot do all that needs to be done. The need is not in itself a calling to do something.

God's practical wisdom in this realm is summarized in this proverb: 'Better is a handful of quietness than two hands full of toil and a striving after wind' (Ecclesiastes 4:6, RSV). Why do we find it so difficult to put this advice into practice? There are several common reasons:

We feel guilty about saying 'no'

No one likes having to refuse a proposal or a request, yet learning to say 'no' is an essential requisite in life and particularly in Christian ministry. If you never say 'no,' you will soon have to say, 'Sorry, I can't because I'm exhausted.' The word 'yes' is very powerful, but the word 'no' is very healthy! A 'no' said in the right moment brings forth health and peace as well as ultimately pleasing God.

Our difficulty in saying 'no' often comes from a desire to please others. We believe that a 'no' could lead to the loss of their love or affection. That is a mistake we need to correct. Trying to please others all the time is like a highway towards exhaustion. God's commandment is to serve and to love our neighbour, not to please them! Pleasing others should never be a priority in our ministry because Jesus himself warned, 'Woe to you when everyone speaks well of you' (Luke 6:26). Recognition from others is valuable, but it should never become the main guide in our decisions. The goal of our life and ministry is to fulfil God's will, not to satisfy people's demands. We must learn to say 'no' without feeling guilty.

We fall victim to dispersion

Dispersion, or a lack of clear goals and objectives, is a frequent cause of activism. We need to take time to plan a 'road map' to avoid taking wrong ways. This was one of the reasons why Jesus could accomplish so many things in such a short time. Jesus had very clear objectives from the beginning. A distinct sense of purpose and direction led him to act at all times within a carefully prepared framework. No wonder he could pray with great satisfaction just before his death, 'I have brought you glory on earth by finishing the work you gave me to do' (John 17:4).

The advice of Oswald Sanders is again helpful here: 'The leader must be meticulously careful in his selection of priorities. . . . If it is his ambition to excel there must be selection and rejection in order to concentrate on the things that are of paramount importance.'[11]

We serve outside of our gifts

It may sound obvious, but we should concentrate our work in those areas where we have received gifts. We have to say 'no' to some opportunities in order to give our best to our priorities. There are few situations when God calls us to a task for which we are not apparently gifted; if he does, it is likely to be for a limited time and after

---

11. Sanders, *Spiritual Leadership*, 87.

a clear calling. The Holy Spirit has poured out different gifts for different services to different people. We should respect this principle of diversity and complementarity in the body of Christ. Serving in areas where we have no gifts causes a lot of extra weariness.

We have a wrong theology of work

We do not live to work, but rather we work to live. If we change the biblical order, we neglect the original purpose of God. Work is an important part of life, but it is not the only one, nor even the most essential one. Work is not an end in itself but a means to serve and glorify God (Colossians 3:22–24).

When work occupies the centre of life, it easily becomes an addiction. The workaholic Christian leader may suffer emotional problems (perfectionism, poor self-esteem, etc), but behind these factors there are always wrong concepts, especially a misinterpretation of the stewardship God has given us. God certainly wants his servants to work with excellence and diligence, but not at the risk of neglecting 'what is better' (remember Jesus' reproach to Martha) that he has also given us to fulfil. Doing things well is important, but for God being comes before doing. Our ultimate calling is not to work more and more, but to become more and more like the Lord of the work.

III. Self-Ambition: The Mistake of Trying to Make a Name for Ourselves

This third mistake is often unconscious, like a blind spot in our vision. It is not easy to acknowledge that we have a problem with vanity, desire for prominence or any wrong motivations. We are not aware of such sins because they remain hidden under the appearance of legitimate service. Sadly, in some cases of fatigue the root cause is too much self-love and too little real love for Christ.

Self-love acts like an ambitious tyrant, insatiable with its demands, draining all our energy and leading finally to the empty pool condition. Be careful with the pervasive narcissism around; it may easily entangle us and lead us astray from our true calling. The end of the story of Narcissus is a useless life, wasted in the slavery of self-centredness and self-love. We should regularly remind ourselves that we are serving the Almighty God, not the little god we all have in our heart.

Three practical exercises will help us avoid self-ambition:

- Cleaning our motivations

- Reviewing our concept of success

- Understanding the value of results

Cleaning our motivations: 'Shine, Jesus, shine'

First of all, we need regularly to clean our motivations. In the same way that washing our hands is a sign of hygiene, washing our motivations in ministry is a sign of spiritual hygiene.

The Babel spirit is almost as old as the human heart: '. . . so that we may make a name for ourselves' (Genesis 11:4). Baruch, Jeremiah's personal assistant, had a similar longing: 'Should you then seek great things for yourself? Do not seek them' (Jeremiah 45:5). God's response to Baruch is a serious warning because 'no one can serve two masters' (Matthew 6:24). Our ambition is either for God or for ourselves. Either we magnify Christ's name or we exalt our own. Christian work is an instrument to accomplish God's global purposes, not a means to build our personal prestige or reputation.

'My joy and my crown': A legitimate sense of fulfilment

Of course, there is a kind of personal fulfilment that is not wrong, but instead it pleases God. It is the legitimate satisfaction that we gain from the work we do. We can fully enjoy the rewards of Christian work in the same way that the Creator rejoiced after finishing his creative deeds (Genesis 1:31).

This was surely the spirit behind Paul's spontaneous exclamation: 'My brothers and sisters . . . my joy and my crown' (Philippians 4:1). Without any embarrassment, the apostle was referring to the Philippian brethren as if they were his personal victory! Is this too arrogant or self-centred? No, the apostle's crystal-clear motivation was never self-fulfilment, but Christ being exalted through his life (Philippians 1:20–21). Notice how he once summed up his ministry: 'And they praised God because of me' (Galatians 1:24). What a marvellous life summary for any Christian worker!

'Do not boast beyond limit': *Soli Deo gloria*

Therefore we should not go beyond this legitimate fulfilment. 'We do not boast beyond limit,' Paul said (2 Corinthians 10:15, RSV). We could say that there is such a thing as a 'permitted boasting,' which is boasting within limits. What limits? 'Not to us, LORD, not to us but to your name be the glory' (Psalm 115:1). The satisfaction may be for me, but the glory is for the Lord. The Reformers emphasized this principle with the memorable dictum *soli Deo gloria* (for God's glory alone). What is at stake in our Christian ministry is neither our prestige nor our self-esteem, but God's glory and reputation.

Being free from the tyranny of self-love and self-fulfilment brings rest and peace to our ministry. When we can heartily exclaim, 'Shine, Jesus, shine, because your name and not mine is what really matters,' then we are delivered from three common dangers:

- The pressure of perfectionism (the compulsive worker)

- The self-centredness of individualism (the lone-ranger worker)

- The coldness of professionalism (the hired-hand worker)

Reviewing our concept of success

We all dream about a successful ministry. No one likes failure, but what are success and failure in God's eyes? What is a successful ministry? The answer to these questions contains a very important key to living a quiet life and accomplishing a work according to God's heart. This is the second exercise that will deliver us from the tyranny of self-ambition.

What is success for our society? The world measures success or failure using mainly three parameters: action, visible results, and image (outward appearance). For this reason its emphases are on activism (doing a lot), on productivity (getting a lot done) and on social status (being able to spend a lot). The core of success lies in quantity and public image. Identity comes from activity. Incidentally, here we have one of the reasons why so many people today fall into depression when they retire. The end of their activity means the end of their identity.

We are not called to be successful, but to be fruitful

God's view differs radically from the world's. The emphasis in the Bible is not on doing a lot, but on *being* more holy; it is not on productivity, but on stewardship; it does not look at the outward appearance, but at the heart. Identity does not come from activity, but from belonging (being in Christ). For God, the core of success lies in attitudes and inner values; it is not a matter of getting many results but of working with the right principles, or building with the right materials (gold, silver, costly stones), as Paul so richly describes in 1 Corinthians 3:10–13. The warning is, 'Let each man take care how he builds' (v. 10, RSV). In accordance with this advice, the essential question in evaluating our work is 'How am I building?' not 'What am I achieving?'

This idea is evident also in the teaching of Jesus. In the parable of the talents (Matthew 25:14–30) his words of praise focus on the faithfulness of the servant, not on the financial gain of the investment! In this parable the Lord commends the essential attitudes of a good steward, attitudes that we can apply to a good minister. The features of a successful minister are faithfulness, diligence and obedience.

What then is 'being fruitful'? It is primarily a matter of growing into the image of Christ, the forging of a Christlike character (Romans 8:29). The texts which refer to our fruit as Christians emphasize character rather than action: 'This is to my

Father's glory, that you bear much fruit, showing yourselves to be my disciples. . . . Now remain in my love' (John 15:8–9). We see the same idea with the fruit of the Spirit in Galatians 5:22–23, where a way of being and behaving is portrayed. Bearing fruit has to do primarily with holiness, not with numbers. This leads us to consider the value of results.

Understanding the value of results

To have a right view of results is the third exercise that will free us from the tyranny of self-ambition (and perfectionism and activism). We should not minimize the value of results because God indeed cares about them. But the Scriptures show that, in a fallen world, results can be neither the primary measure of work nor an expression of the worker's quality. Many servants of God would be considered failures if judged by the criteria of society. The work of patriarchs, prophets and even some of the apostles were far from 'successful' ministries.

Consider the list of the heroes of faith in Hebrews 11. I have always found it striking and encouraging that some of the names on this glorious record were clearly losers, not winners, according to the world's standards. This 'honour list' even includes anonymous life wanderers: 'They went about in sheepskins and goatskins, destitute, persecuted and mistreated—the world was not worthy of them.

They wandered in deserts and mountains, living in caves and in holes in the ground' (Hebrews 11:36–38).

The eyes of faith look at success in life from a different perspective, a perspective that takes into account two realities.

'Sowing and reaping': Our perception is very limited

Results in Christian work are like an iceberg: what we see is only a tiny part of the whole. It is significant that the illustration Jesus chose for Christian work is that of the sower. Sowing and reaping always contain an element of uncertainty and even mystery. When we sow the seed of the gospel, there is a much deeper reality hidden from our sight that only God knows and, eventually, time will reveal to us. Our eyes only see the 'here and now', but the eyes of faith reach far beyond and contemplate reality from the view of eternity. Notice the beatitude in Revelation 14:13: 'Blessed are the dead who die in the Lord from now on . . . they will rest from their labour, for their deeds will follow them.' The emphasis is on 'their deeds'—what they *did*—not on their successes—what they achieved.

There will be many surprises in heaven. Those the world calls 'losers' will be the winners greatly praised by the Lord of the work. This is what God reminds us through the psalmist: 'Those who sow with tears will reap with songs of joy' (Psalm 126:5).

'Thorns and thistles': Coping with frustration and disappointment

The Fall caused the whole creation to be subject to *frustration* (Romans 8:20). This word is quite similar to the modern idea of disappointment. It is important for us to grasp its full meaning because disappointment—unfulfilled desires or expectations—and frustration are common experiences in Christian ministry. We need to learn how to cope with them.

Frustration is an experience of emptiness and grief when you have invested a lot of time and effort with someone or some project but the results are poor or negligible. You did your best but you got the worst. Have you ever felt this way? If so, do not feel alone. God himself had this sort of experience with his people, vividly described in the Song of the Vineyard: 'What more could have been done for my vineyard than I have done for it? When I looked for good grapes, why did it yield only bad?' (Isaiah 5:4). I find great comfort in this passage whenever I experience some disappointment because I feel understood by God himself.

God's frustration with his people—and our frustration too—have to do with the 'thorns and thistles' that the Earth produced after the Fall. Work already existed in God's creation and it was good and pleasant. But sin brought forth two main changes: the circumstances of work became hard—'the sweat of your brow' was introduced; and the results were also affected—'thorns and thistles' appeared for the first time. In a fallen world bad results are not necessarily related to poor work or a deficient worker. Excellent work can yield 'bad grapes.' If this happened to the Lord of the vineyard, how much more it can happen to the workers of the vineyard!

It is also important to note that frustration and guilt are not the same. Sometimes we say 'I feel guilty' when what we really mean is 'I feel frustrated.' It is important to discern between these to avoid the unnecessary burden of false guilt. When you do something wrong, either making a mistake or committing a sin, guilt is the appropriate reaction. True guilt correlates with wrongdoing. An objective fault can be identified. On the other hand, when you have done your best but things go wrong, you may feel frustrated, but you should not feel guilty. The results have gone wrong, but you have done things rightly, like in the Song of the Vineyard.

This misconception is quite common in Christian ministry, especially among evangelists, because the awareness of the needs of the unreached burdens their heart. This is a good and holy reaction, but the feeling that they (preachers) are guilty if people go to hell is not a right one. Christians are called to be messengers and ambassadors, not demigods; the results of our proclamation belong to God. Ours is the ministry of preaching, but to the Holy Spirit alone belongs the ministry of convicting of sin (John 16:8). Our heart may be sad and grieved—frustrated—by the lack of results, like Jesus was when he wept over Jerusalem (Luke 19:41), but this frustration is an expression of maturity and pleases God. Don't feel guilty!

IV. Haste: The Mistake of Never Slowing Down

This last factor is actually an outcome of the previous mistakes. When you work under too much pressure, either because you are overcommitted, because you are a compulsive perfectionist or because you are driven by self-ambition, then you will likely live hurriedly.

Working a lot can be tiring, but working under haste is draining. Haste affects us (and also those around us) because when we are in a hurry, we never give the impression that we care. A still heart conveys gentleness and sweetness, whereas a hurried person conveys rudeness and even aggressiveness. The Swiss psychiatrist Karl Jung rightly said: 'Hurry is not of the devil, it is the devil'!

Jesus lived a very intensive life; he worked hard and he never wasted a minute. Yet we never see him in a hurry except when he had to flee from temptation (John 6:15). There is indeed a lot of action in our Lord's life, but he maintained a serene, quiet pace. We see no pause and no hurry in his ministry. The 'slow movement' is not an invention of the twenty-first century, but is the rhythm of life that

God intended for his creation, where everything has its right time (Ecclesiastes 3:1).

If you drive a car too fast, you are more likely to have an accident. The same thing happens with the driving of our life. The faster we live, the more likely we are to have undesired life events.

'Be alert': The spiritual battle, an extra cause of weariness

'When you do not pray, you are an easy prey.'[12]

We cannot close here; a key factor is missing. Every Christian leader suffers an extra cause of weariness that goes beyond the natural or human dimensions considered so far. Our work is not an ordinary work; it is God's work. This is why it is subject to the same opposition Jesus had to face. We make a mistake if we overlook the spiritual battle we are immersed in. There is a supernatural dimension in our fatigue, 'for our struggle is not against flesh and blood, but . . . against the powers of this dark world and against the spiritual forces of evil in the heavenly realms' (Ephesians 6:12).

This is why Jesus warned Peter, 'Satan has asked to sift all of you as wheat. But I have prayed for you, Simon, that your faith may not fail' (Luke 22:31–32). The Lord knew Bounds' thought well:

---

12. E M Bounds, *The Power of Prayer,* One Minute Devotions (Bloomingdale, IL: Christian Art Gifts, 2007), November 15.

'When you do not pray, you are an easy prey.' Peter later warned all of us, 'Be alert and of sober mind. Your enemy the devil prowls around like a roaring lion looking for someone to devour' (1 Peter 5:8). The awareness of God's presence makes us strong, but the awareness of the devil's presence makes us wisely alert.

Because our weariness ultimately has to do with a spiritual battle, we need to rest in God, our source of strength. This is essential if we are to guard our vineyard properly, for 'if God is for us, who can be against us?' (Romans 8:31).

Chapter 4

Guarding Your Vineyard: The Practice of Caring for Yourself

'Therefore we do not lose heart. Though outwardly we are wasting away, yet inwardly we are being renewed day by day.'

2 Corinthians 4:16

What an encouraging statement! Paul suffered weariness and fatigue more than any of us. Yet, according to this verse, he knew how to receive fresh strength every day. He was confident about the secret of renewal, and the same resources he used to thrive and survive in his outstanding ministry are available for us.

So far we have seen mistakes and dangers to avoid. Now let us turn these warnings into constructive strategies: What can we do to put principles into practice, and thus prevent the empty pool syndrome? How can we implement the care of ourselves?

We leave the illustration of the pool and turn back to a rich biblical metaphor: the vineyard. Our life can be compared to a vineyard—or a garden—where we are the gardeners, though not the owners. As we will see in the next chapter, God is the Chief

Gardener, the owner of the vineyard. We should not forget this at any time because it conveys an important two-fold message: (i) it gives us a sense of responsibility—we are called to be good stewards of this vineyard; and (ii) it is a source of great relief—we are not alone in the care of the garden. God is guiding and helping us in all our labours. We are indeed responsible for the management of our lives—there is work to do—but God is watching over us. We ultimately rest in the Chief Gardener.

What are our duties in guarding the vineyard?

Guarding Our Emotional and Spiritual Wellbeing

'They made me keeper of the vineyards; but my own vineyard I have not kept!' (Song of Songs 1:6b, RSV)

Three main practices will help you keep your garden. These should be done regularly and with discipline.

- Pruning: learning to renounce

- Watering: learning to renew yourself

- Waiting: learning to be patient

Pruning: Learning to renounce

'Less means more.'[13]

Good gardeners have to prune if they want their trees and plants to bear fruit. Likewise, we should learn to do less in order to grow more.

Christian leaders, as we said earlier, are usually multi-gifted people who are able to do many things well. This is why they find it difficult to say 'no' to areas of ministry which they enjoy and, for some time, do very capably. Dispersion, though, is a subtle enemy, acting often as a silent 'killer.' It penetrates your life insidiously—you are unaware of its danger—and it drains your energy little by little until one day you suddenly realize you are unable to enjoy what you are doing and you feel like giving everything up. It has wearied you physically, emotionally and, consequently, spiritually. The inability to renounce tasks or responsibilities leads to dispersion and dispersion leads to defeat.

Pruning—renouncing—in our ministry may imply two kinds of decisions: choosing and changing.

Choosing

Life is a constant exercise of choosing. The difficulty comes when the choice is between the good

---

13. Ludwig Mies Van Der Rohe (1886–1969) is the main advocate in architecture for what is known as *minimalism*.

and the best. Choosing, then, means renouncing, and this is not an easy thing to do because there is an element of sacrifice in it. Renouncing means sacrificing those 'good things' that may be distractions in the fulfilment of our ministry. We need the courage to sacrifice some legitimate opportunities in order to focus on our priorities.

Changing

Sometimes pruning means change. We need to be ready to make changes in our life. Occasionally a big, radical change may be required. There are times of reorientation in our calling and ministry, changes which necessarily involve a 'big move'; for example, going to live in another place or starting a different sort of ministry. Some big changes should be considered if you have been under permanent stress for months. This is a sign that something is wrong and needs to be corrected. Emotional exhaustion is always an opportunity to discover areas in our life that require transformation.

Most times, however, the changes are small adjustments. Fatigue is often caused by poor organization in the areas of time and administration. Christian workers are usually very good in dealing with people and ideas, but not with things. Often they do not have the gift of administration! We need help there. Small changes in these areas can eventually bring forth big outcomes. One of the best ways to prevent fatigue is order, which can greatly enhance our efficiency and help us work in a relaxed way. An orderly life is a source of wellbeing whereas disorder, at all levels, is a major source of stress.

Our schedules, for example, can be really unhealthy! As a psychiatrist, I have been surprised time and again to see how Christian leaders often fail in those areas that we consider obvious, like making an appointment for a regular medical check-up. We are ready to advise others about the priority of health—we take good care of others' vineyards—yet we fail to apply the same zeal to our own lives!

We greatly, and rightly, emphasize the need for a holy life, but forget too often the need for a healthy lifestyle. Holiness and health are equally God's original design for us. One of the favourite thoughts of Hans Bürki, a former IFES leader and writer, was: 'Reduce, renounce, simplify.' If you put it into practice, you will discover how helpful, and indeed how healthy, this advice is to your ministry.

Watering: Learning to renew yourself

> *'You will be like a well-watered garden, like a spring whose waters never fail.'* (Isaiah 58:11)

The pruning shears are not enough to keep the vineyard in shape. We also need water. Watering is the key activity if the plants are to stay fresh and alive. If pruning strengthens the tree, water provides revitalization. When water is lacking, dryness follows, but a 'well-watered garden' will likely bear much fruit. (Remember the vivid descriptions in Psalm 1 and Psalm 92:12–14.) The same happens in the vineyard of our ministry.

The key question here is how we can become 'like a well-watered garden, like a spring whose waters never fail.'

Our renewal essentially comes from relationships. As John Donne, the great metaphysical poet, wrote, 'No man is an island.' God made us relational beings. Paramount for our renewal is the relationship with him, the 'spring of water welling up to eternal life' (John 4:14), so we will devote the next chapter entirely to this. There are five other kinds of relationships available to the Christian leader. These are fresh water to us, absolutely vital in our ministry and life.

i. The relationship with our family

God uses the members of the family to provide support and renewal to his servants. We truly have duties to our loved ones, spouse, children or parents. Our family, however, should not be seen as another burden—one more area of obligations—but as an oasis, a place to relax and celebrate, a place to be fully ourselves. A supportive family is a great antidote against weariness.

Several examples in the Bible confirm the value of the family in the ministry of God's servants. The extended family of Moses is a fine illustration, despite their occasional mistakes and sins. From the very beginning, when Moses' sister played a decisive role in saving his life as a baby (Exodus 2:4–10), till the end when his brother Aaron held his hands up (Exodus 17:12), his family was a means of support to him. How encouraging to see that God uses imperfect families to support his servants!

Learn to relax and be refreshed with your family. This is a powerful counterbalance to the stress of ministry. Laughing, playing, talking, sharing, reading, praying, going for outings, and being able to enjoy the little blessings and joys of everyday life together all act as a balm to the demands of ministry. By engaging with your family you do a lot of good to them and to yourself.

I will never forget how, when I was seven or eight years old, my father, a busy pastor of a large church, set aside a few minutes to play football with me almost every day! Likewise, the outings we had as a family on Mondays, his free day, conveyed a clear and memorable message to me: 'My parents have time for me, and they enjoy being with me.' And years later, when I was an adult, my father told me, 'These times were not an obligation but a celebration for me!'

A fruitful ministry always begins at home. If we are able to create an atmosphere of joy and peace at home, regaining a little of the 'playing spirit'[14] that

---

14. The role and value of playing was first thoroughly researched by the Dutch thinker Johan Huizinga in his book *Homo Ludens* (Madrid: Alianza Editorial, 1972).

we all keep from childhood, our family will be a spring of fresh water for us and, at the same time, we will be a blessing to them. Let us remember that, in this sense, the family is part of our ministry too. To minister is to serve and the first place we are called to be servants is our family. In terms of serving, there is no dichotomy between ministry and family. When you spend time with your spouse or children, even leisure time, you are indeed ministering to them. If you want to be a good minister, start with your loved ones.

ii. The relationship with our church

It is not surprising that David wrote, 'I rejoiced with those who said to me, "Let us go to the house of the LORD"' (Psalm 122:1). Fellowship with our brothers and sisters is 'good and pleasant' (Psalm 133:1), a source of joy and renewal that we should not neglect. Try to be in your local church for as many Sundays as you can. There will be times when this isn't possible if you travel often, but try to work your schedule so you can be there. This will give you an anchor for your spiritual life and service, and it will be easier for others to pray for you if they can get to know you. Let's reflect often on that metaphor of Christ's body on earth so we grasp more and more deeply what it means. It is to the church that Christ has entrusted his commission, and from the church that we receive our commission. While the nature of your ministry may make it more difficult to join service rotations, go with a serving spirit, ready to, in the rich words of the Anglican liturgy, 'hear and receive God's holy word,' prepared to minister to others in conversation and ready for them to minister to you.

iii. The relationship with close friends

Friends play a key role in our inner renewal. Jesus himself had a more intimate circle of three people within the group of disciples: he used to take Peter, John and James to share some of the highlights of his life, both the glorious ones like the transfiguration and the ominous ones like Gethsemane. A similar relationship with Mary, Martha and Lazarus made possible many refreshment hours at their house in Bethany. No doubt their friendship contributed a lot to our Lord's wellbeing and renewal.

Likewise Paul often refers to the special meaning that fellow workers like Timothy, Epaphroditus, Luke or Titus, among others, had in his life and ministry. Their faithful support was a strategic tool used by the Holy Spirit to greatly enhance his influential leadership.

Loneliness is one of the greatest enemies of the Christian leader. Most leaders' moral failures occur when they are incubated in isolation and loneliness. You cannot be 'a rock' on which others can depend if you are also 'an island.'[15] As Simon and Garfunkel

---

15. 'I Am a Rock' and 'The Sound of Silence' are songs by Simon and Garfunkel, popular singers in the 1960s and 1970s.

remind us: 'silence like a cancer grows.' Isolation weakens the Christian worker in many ways and contributes to the draining of their energies. It is much more difficult—and not right—to try to thrive and survive as a lone ranger in ministry. The reason is not simply an emotional one. Friends are one of the main tools God uses to keep his servants steadfast before the attacks of the enemy.

Notice that the exhortation to 'carry each other's burdens' (Galatians 6:2) occurs in the context of moral failure and restoration (6:1). Persistent loneliness is a risk factor in Christian leadership, as sadly evidenced by the fall of some popular figures in the evangelical world. Falls and failures are best prevented by support and accountability.

For this reason, I earnestly recommend that you build support and accountability relationships by creating a small group (two or three people) and meeting with them regularly (at least once or twice a year). I remember John Stott referring to the immense value of his own small group of support. He called them his 'advisory group of elders' (AGE). These small structures become invaluable if you want to prevent both burnout and moral failure. When you can share and discuss your burdens, your problems and your priorities, you feel supported and at the same time make yourself accountable for your actions. I like to call it 'the divine triangle': sharing, accountability and support; in contrast with the devil's triangle: loneliness, isolation and individualism.

iv. The relationship with nature

It cannot be mere coincidence that God placed the first humans in a garden. Nature endows us with harmony and equilibrium. We have all experienced the invigorating effect of a long walk in the countryside when we are worried or tense. The old Romans summed up the positive effects of walking in the phrase *solvitur ambulando* ('you solve it by walking'). Indeed, how often we perceive a problem in a different way after a brisk stroll!

In a world where the whole creation is 'groaning' (Romans 8:22), we should neither idolize nor idealize nature. This is the mistake some trendy philosophies and Eastern forms of spirituality make today. Nature itself saves nobody, but it does bring us closer to the Creator and renew us physically and mentally. From William Carey (a notable gardening enthusiast) to John Stott (a keen ornithologist), numerous servants of God have found in nature one of the keys to their personal renovation and equilibrium. On a personal note, I try to put this advice into practice by going for a stroll for an hour three or four times a week, which can be surprisingly helpful.

v. The relationship with books

Last but not least! Reading is an excellent source of personal renewal. We are not referring here to the word of God, the Book par excellence (which we will consider later), but to our supplementary reading. From his request to Timothy, we know that books were important for Paul: 'When you come, bring . . . the books, and above all the parchments' (2 Timothy 4:13, RSV). Some books become like friends.

Reading is a sort of dialogue, a personal silent dialogue that provides refreshment and even healing. The American psychoanalyst Karl Menninger recommended to his patients the practice of 'bibliotherapy', healing through reading. Whether the reading is for pleasure or for study, the pages of a book open new landscapes to our life and help us water our vineyard.

From the last two relationships, nature and books, we see that having specific times to be on our own (besides our quiet times with the Lord) is a necessary part of renewal. Some temperaments need this more than others: introverts, for example, usually recharge their 'batteries' by being on their own; whereas the more extroverted you are, the more you need contact with other people to get new energy![16] Persistent loneliness has risks, but some time on our own provides the right environment for rest and refreshment.

Developing and enjoying these five relationships will surely prevent many mistakes in your life. If you regularly practice them 'you will be like

---

16. For a more detailed study, see Pablo Martinez, *Praying with the Grain: How Your Personality Affects the Way You Pray* (Oxford: Monarch Books, 2012).

a well-watered garden, like a spring whose waters never fail' (Isaiah 58:11).

Waiting: Learning to be patient

> 'Be patient . . . until the Lord's coming. See how the farmer waits for the land to yield its valuable crop, patiently waiting for the autumn and spring rains.' (James 5:7)

Patience is another trait of the good gardener. In the same way that the farmer has to wait 'for the autumn and spring rains,' the Christian worker needs to learn the value of waiting. Why is it important? Lack of patience increases our weariness and often makes us pick fruit when it is not yet ripe, leading us to make decisions in the wrong season. A meaningful percentage of mistakes in Christian ministry arise from not understanding—or accepting—that God's calendar is different from ours. We work with months and years (*kronos*); God works according to the right season, the suitable opportunity (*kairos*).

The biblical concept of waiting is much richer than our definition, and it widens our understanding of how we should wait. It conveys two attitudes that define patience:

- Trust: A still heart. Do not be anxious.

- Searching: Eyes wide open. Be alert like the watchman on his tower.

This is not an easy attitude in a society that worships all that is instant and quick. Modern society adores the immediate and rejects all that requires pausing or waiting. Christian ministry is not free from the pressure of immediacy, which has become an idol, and this can badly distort the way we evaluate success or failure.

We are called to be like oaks, not mushrooms!

God is not interested so much in immediate visible results as in 'fruit that remains,' as we anticipated in chapter three. The illustration of the oak tree and the mushroom help us understand this principle. A mushroom grows very quickly—just one night is enough to have a beautiful, grown mushroom—yet you can easily pick it because it has no roots. Quick growth, nice appearance, but very fragile—the life of a mushroom is ephemeral.

The oak, on the other hand, grows steadily and slowly with a distinctive feature: all that grows on the surface is reflected in its depth; its roots are as deep as its height. To pluck an oak is impossible. Steady growth, strong roots, long life—God wants our ministries to be like oaks, not mushrooms!

Hope is the foundation of patience

Notice how James relates patience to the second coming of the Lord: 'Be patient, then, brothers and sisters, until the Lord's coming' (James 5:7). Patience and hope are inseparably linked. A still waiting is not possible without a firm hope, the glorious hope of the parousia. True rest and renewal ultimately come from our future hope. This hope makes us strong and helps us persevere in the midst of 'outwardly wasting away.' This is the core of our inner renewal and the reason why we 'do not lose heart' (2 Corinthians 4:16).

Chapter 5

'Be Still, and Know That I Am God': The Healthiest Renewal

'"Go out and stand on the mountain in the presence of the LORD, for the LORD is about to pass by". . . . But the LORD was not in the fire. And after the fire came a gentle whisper. . . . Then a voice said to him, "What are you doing here, Elijah?"'

1 Kings 19:11–13

Many Christian workers are very good at 'cooking' for others, but they neglect to 'cook' for themselves. They readily prepare excellent spiritual food for their congregation, but they hardly go to the Bible for their own needs and spiritual pleasure. This is a common mistake and a great loss. The lack of personal spiritual nourishment causes progressive weakening and weariness leading eventually to a neglected, dry vineyard.

Diligence to provide for your own spiritual nourishment is a necessary qualification for leadership. Paul made it clear to Timothy: 'You will be a good minister of Christ Jesus, nourished on the truths of the faith and of the good teaching that you have followed' (1 Timothy 4:6). If you fail at this point, your whole ministry is likely to fail. Notice that Paul's warning is followed some verses later by the advice, 'take care of yourself' (see v. 16). The first step in taking care of yourself is to be spiritually well nourished.

Our relationship with God provides the main spring of fresh water in our renewal. Being with our loved ones, enjoying Christian fellowship, nature and books—all these relationships are very refreshing, but they are not enough. Our fundamental rest and renewal come from our fellowship with the living God through Jesus Christ. There are some spiritual and emotional demands in Christian ministry that only God can fill, for they are God-shaped needs. Our renewal requires a supernatural strength that goes beyond natural or human means.

Spiritual renewal that comes from fellowship with God is paramount for any Christian leader because:

- It is a vital connection: 'Apart from me you can do nothing' (John 15:5).

- It is what Jesus did and taught us to do: 'Come ye yourselves apart' (Mark 6:31, KJV).

- It is a requisite to feed Christ's flock: 'Feed my lambs' (John 21:15).

'Apart from Me You Can Do Nothing': A Vital Connection

'Remain in me, as I also remain in you. . . . I am the vine; you are the branches. If you remain in me and I in you, you will bear much fruit.'
(John 15:4–5)

Spiritual renewal is paramount, first of all, because we need a connection with Christ. I think it is no accident that Jesus uses the illustration of the vineyard to explain it. 'No branch can bear fruit by itself. . . . Apart from me you can do nothing' (John 15:4–5). The Lord is very emphatic: it is a matter of life and death. In the same way that the branch needs the sap, we need the spiritual energy, the divine sap that only Christ can provide. Neither a Christian nor any Christian ministry can survive apart from the constant renewal that comes from God.

Our connection with Christ implies also a vital connection with the Scriptures because Christ is the center of all the Scriptures (Luke 24:27). We encounter God in the word of God, not through abstract or empty meditation. The psalmist describes this idea with the illustration, once more, of the well-watered tree. Psalm 1, a favourite song for many Christian workers, says:

> Blessed is the one . . . whose delight is in the law of the LORD, and who meditates on his law day and night. That person is like a tree planted by

streams of water, which yields its fruit in season and whose leaf does not wither; whatever
they do prospers. (vv. 2–3)

Psalm 46 widens our vision by giving us a hint
on the 'how' of this connection: 'Be still, and know
that I am God' (v. 10). Some quietness is necessary.
Notice the link between 'being still' and 'knowing
God.' It is through quietness that we 'know' (per-
sonally experience) God. Of course this is not the
only way to encounter him, but by 'being still'[17] we
can best listen to his voice and thus experience
inner renewal. Elijah did not hear God's voice in the
wind, in the earthquake or in the fire. God was not
there. The exhausted prophet could only hear God's
voice through a gentle whisper, 'on the mountain in
the presence of the LORD' (1 Kings 19:11).

Only in God's presence can we breathe God's
breath and receive God's strength.

The context of Psalm 46 reminds us of a striking paradox: when we are still, God is a strength
to us. This is why the psalm begins joyfully, 'God
is our refuge and strength, an ever-present help
in trouble.' This is a constant feature of Christian
life and ministry: in our weakness, God becomes
a mighty fortress. No wonder these exultant words
inspired Martin Luther to compose the memorable hymn 'A Mighty Fortress Is Our God.' The
more distressed you are, the more you need to rest

---

17. The word 'still' here may also convey the idea of
'surrender,' therefore implying trust.

in God, because God's 'power is made perfect in weakness' (2 Corinthians 12:9).

This vital connection bestows a divine provision with five fundamental ingredients of renewal. They are the divine remedy against the symptoms of the empty pool considered in chapter two. When we are still before God we receive:

- Deep rest that relieves our inner unrest

- New strength that relieves our fatigue and lack of motivation

- Fresh guidance that relieves our anxiety

- Complete joy that relieves our disappointments

- A firm hope that relieves our weariness and dismay

It provides us with deep rest

> 'My Presence will go with you, and I will give you rest.' (Exodus 33:14)

Moses had a supportive family but he claimed God's presence with him as a condition to start his tough ministry as a leader: 'Then Moses said to him, "If your Presence does not go with us, do not send us up from here"' (Exodus 33:15). He knew very well that leading God's people is a demanding task which requires constant renewal. Moses had to learn that resting in God means developing the awareness of God's presence. This does not imply feeling God, but being conscious of the reality that God is with us and within us.

Psalm 23, one of the best-known poems in the world, shows this connection in a beautiful metaphor. The Lord, the shepherd, is a source of green pastures and quiet waters. Being with him 'refreshes my soul.' In just two verses the link between rest and God's leading (presence) is repeated three times. If we truly experience that 'The LORD is my shepherd, I shall not want,' then every anxiety, burden or problem in our ministry is contemplated with inner rest in spite of the hostility outside (v. 5).

What kind of rest is divine rest? It is not a vague feeling of wellbeing or a mental detachment from suffering, but liberation from specific burdens, like heavy baggage being unloaded. Notice the context of the promise, 'Come to me, all you who are weary and burdened, and I will give you rest' (Matthew 11:28). Jesus was referring to the burden of legalism imposed by the Pharisees. Jesus' rest delivers us from the tyranny of perfectionism, from the disappointment of poor visible results, from any guilt—true or false—about our doings, from the anxiety of church problems, from the pain of conflict in relationships, from the wounds of ingratitude, from the weariness of running a tiring race.

We can be renewed by Christ's rest in all these circumstances if we remember that:

- He is with us (Matthew 28:20)
- He understands us (Hebrews 4:15)
- He intercedes for us (Hebrews 7:25)
- He provides a way out to every trial (1 Corinthians 10:13)

An illustration by Henry Drummond vividly describes the uniqueness of the rest we find in Christ.

The robin's nest under the waterfall: True rest in Christ

'Two artists each painted a picture to illustrate his conception of rest. The first chose for his scene a still, lone lake among the far-off mountains. . . . But the second artist, on his canvas, wildly painted a thundering waterfall. . . . A closer look revealed a fragile birch tree bending over the mist of the roaring water. At the fork of the branch, wet with spray, there sat a robin on its nest.' —Henry Drummond

The first painting was only stagnant. . . . But the second . . . truly described what it means to rest. For in rest, there are always two elements, right: tranquility and energy; silence and turbulence; creation and destruction; fearlessness and fearfulness. And it was the same way with Christ.[18]

---

18. Joni Eareckson Tada, "Real Rest," 5 February 2014, transcript and audio, 3:59, Joni and Friends Radio Program, http://www.joniandfriends.org/radio/4-minute/real-rest/.

It is a source of new strength

> '*In repentance and rest is your salvation, in quietness and trust is your strength.*' (Isaiah 30:15)

This verse from Isaiah brings a promise and a challenge at the same time! God wants his people to find their strength in quietness and trust. It is an encouraging promise because new strength is guaranteed, but it is a great challenge too because our natural tendency is to search for strength in action, not in reflection. Notice how rest, trust and new strength go together like a refreshing cluster. To rest upon the Lord is an expression of trust. For God—and his servants—the supreme source of strength lies in quietness before him. In this sense, activism may be a symptom of weakness rather than strength, whereas the quietness that comes from trust is a sign of spiritual maturity.

Therefore, being still before God is an exercise of trust that supplies us with both rest and strength. This refreshing association is often mentioned in the Scriptures. For example, in Psalm 23 again, the phrase 'He refreshes my soul' can also be translated 'He renews my inner life' or 'He restores my strength.' The same principle is declared in Isaiah: 'Those who hope in the LORD will renew their strength' (Isaiah 40:31).

Likewise Paul asserts: 'I can *do* all this through him who gives me strength' (Philippians 4:13). Paul did not mean that in Christ we become like 'superman', a sort of omnipotent person that can do everything. It is worth noting that the verb 'to do' does not occur in the original text, so the idea is rather: 'I can be stronger than any problem or situation, and I can overcome everything when I am in Christ'. Notice again the vital connection with Christ.

It is a source of guidance

> 'I will instruct you and teach you in the way you should go; I will counsel you with my loving eye on you.' (Psalm 32:8)

It is in God's presence that we receive discernment and new light. Any problem, conflict, decision or project gets a new perspective under his direction. We get from him the instruction for our daily life as well as for important decisions and plans.

God's gentle whisper enables us to discern between the important and the urgent, the essential and the secondary. It is an invaluable tool in our planning. It sharpens our priorities, provides a global vision to our daily activities and reminds us of the bigger framework of our work, which goes beyond the here and now to reach eternity. When we put our life under the gaze of God, we find, like Teresa of Avila, that 'the divine inner words are produced in the soul at moments when it is incapable of understanding them.'[19]

---

19. Quoted by Paul Tournier in *Técnica psicoanalítica y fe religiosa* (Buenos Aires: La Aurora, 1999), 230.

In God's presence, furthermore, we come to discover the message behind our fatigues, the mistakes, conflicts or deficiencies that are draining our energy. He uncovers those areas of our lives that need repairing or changing. In Paul Tournier's words: 'Those insights which are the most truly fertile . . . are the questions he asks us, not those that we ask him.'[20] His gentle whisper makes our understanding grow progressively till our darkness is turned into light: 'For with you is the fountain of life; in your light we see light' (Psalm 36:9). This gentle guidance relieves our anxiety and uncertainty and makes an important contribution to our inner renewal.

It provides us with complete joy

> 'Do not grieve, for the joy of the Lord is your strength.' (Nehemiah 8:10)

It is remarkable that in Peter's first sermon in Acts, he mentions the link between joy and God's presence. The apostle quotes Psalm 16: 'You have made known to me the paths of life; you will fill me with joy in your presence' (Acts 2:28).

God's presence is a source of joy. Christian joy goes beyond feelings to become a *state,* a condition of deep wellbeing. Joy was the first reaction of the wise men when Jesus was born (Matthew

---

20. Paul Tournier, *Medicina de la Persona* (Pamplona: Editorial Gómez, 1965), 317.

2:10). 'Great joy' was likewise the first reaction of the apostles when Jesus rose from the dead (Luke 24:52). Joy was constantly present in Jesus' life: 'I have told you this so that my joy may be in you and that your joy may be complete' (John 15:11).

Paul's emphasis on where to get joy is no accident: 'Rejoice in the Lord always. I will say it again: Rejoice!' (Philippians 4:4). The spring of joy is, once more, found in a vital connection with Christ.

Joy is indeed an essential trait in the relationship between human beings and their Creator. God always intended fellowship with him to be a pleasure, not a burden! About thirty years ago I was puzzled to find out that 'guilt' was the word Christian leaders most often associated with prayer. Prayer as a 'factory of guilt feelings'? What a tragedy and a loss! This is why I felt the need to write a book on this issue.[21] I expressed the book's purpose like this:

> I would like the reader to think of prayer without guilt. . . . Prayer should not be just one more burden in life, but a pleasure to enjoy . . . Prayer is a powerful tool to bring emotional healing to our lives. It is in prayer that we encounter, face to face, the Supreme Physician, our Lord Jesus Christ, who wants to give us 'life to the full.'

---

21. Martinez, *Praying with the Grain*. Now available in thirteen languages.

When Christian leaders come to experience prayer as a pleasure and not an obligation, a source of joy and not of guilt, the seeds for a powerful Christ-centred leadership are sowed.

Joy is an excellent test to measure the freshness of our ministry. Remaining joyful is an accurate indicator of healthy inner renewal. The joy of Christ is the best 'vaccination' against pessimism and disappointments.

It provides us with a 'firm and secure' hope

> 'So that . . . we who have fled to take hold of the hope set before us may be greatly encouraged. We have this hope as an anchor for the soul, firm and secure.' (Hebrews 6:18–19)

Hope is to the Christian—and especially to the Christian worker—what oxygen is to the lungs. A ministry without hope inevitably leads to dryness. Hope delivers us from weariness and dismay.

What makes our hope firm and secure? Our hope comes from a right vision: 'fixing our eyes on Jesus' (Hebrews 12:2). This vision helps us focus every problem, every burden and every trial in the right perspective: the refreshing glimpse of eternity. It is the key to persevering like Moses 'persevered because he saw him who is invisible' (Hebrews 11:27). What a wondrous paradox that only the eyes of faith make possible!

Moses also 'was looking ahead to his reward' (Hebrews 11:26). How uplifting the vision of the reward is to the Christian leader. We look forward to 'an inheritance that can never perish, spoil or fade. This inheritance is kept in heaven for you' (1 Peter 1:3–4). We also look forward to the promised three-fold crown: the Crown of Life, the Crown of Justice and the Crown of Glory. But above all we long to be with the giver of the crown, our Lord Jesus.

The rest that comes from hope is beautifully expressed by Joni Eareckson Tada:

> How good it will feel for us to be home! . . . No more toiling, no more prying the world's suction cups off my heart. When Hebrews chapter 4, verse 9 describes that Sabbath rest for the people of God, well, it's like a long drink of cool water on a hot day. Maybe the writers of the Bible—some whose joints were stiff from prison chains that chafed . . . had this sweet rest in mind, a rest that perked them up and quickened their pace. Toward the end of their lives, they wrote vigorous encouragements like . . . Hebrews chapter 4, verse 11 where they say, 'Let us, therefore, make every effort to enter that rest.'[22]

---

22. Joni Eareckson Tada, "Enter That Rest," 19 November 2013, transcript and audio, 4:01, Joni and Friends Radio Program, http://www.joniandfriends.org/radio/4-minute/enter-rest/.

Therefore, the renewal that comes from being still and knowing God is manifested in deep rest, new strength, fresh guidance, renewed joy and hope. I cannot think of a better restoration. This is why I called it the healthiest renewal!

'Come Ye Yourselves Apart': The Quiet Times of Jesus, Our Model

'Jesus often withdrew to lonely places and prayed.'
(Luke 5:16)

There is a second reason why spiritual renewal that comes from fellowship with God is paramount: this is what Jesus did and taught us to do. Jesus set the perfect example of what it means to 'be still and know God.' Our Lord was a man of prayer and meditation. This was a major source of power in his ministry.

Rest as a discipline

'Jesus often withdrew to lonely places and prayed.' Both verbs—withdrawing and praying—imply a decision, a firm determination. Rest does not come automatically. It is something you have to pursue. It requires discipline and effort. If you wait passively for the opportunity to rest, it may never come. The blessing of renewal requires the discipline of rest.

A time to give, a time to receive

Why did Jesus need to withdraw from people and draw near to his Father? His own nourishment was at stake. It was in his relationship with his Father that he received; in his relationship with people he gave. Notice again the principle of the two movements here, the need of a constant balance between action and pause, output and input. If this was not a luxury but a matter of spiritual survival for Jesus, it is even more important for us!

Being busy in public ministry requires resting in your private 'monastery'

The busier you are, the more you need to pause and renew. This is what Jesus did with his disciples after a day of hectic activity: 'Come with me by yourselves to a quiet place and get some rest' (Mark 6:31). No wonder that, as we read Christian biographies, we soon find that the giants of faith were men and women of prayer. They simply imitated their Master. Luther, Calvin, Wesley, Carey and many others found in prayer the vital breath of their faith and the source of their strength. Luther, for example, wrote: 'Prayer is a very precious medicine, one that helps and never fails.'[23]

---

23. *Luther's Prayers*, ed. Herbert Brockering (Philadelphia: Fortress, 1994), 40.

The practice of 'being still': Prayer and meditation

How did Jesus spend these times of quietness? He prayed and he was in close fellowship with the Father. Prayer and meditation are the core of 'being still.' Remarkably the transfiguration, one of the highlights of Jesus' life, occurred while he was praying together with three disciples: 'As he was praying, the appearance of his face changed' (Luke 9:29).

Our 'being still' as Christians is almost the opposite of the Eastern forms of meditation. Its purpose is not to reach a certain emotional state, but rather to enjoy an intimate relationship with Jesus Christ in order to become more and more like him (Romans 8:29). We do not want to meet with ourselves, we want to meet with God. Being still before God is not looking inward, introspection, but looking upward, inspiration.

With this purpose in mind, 'the Christian, in his practice of meditation, has a precise map, the word of God, and a visible north, the person of Jesus Christ. Both of these reference points keep the Christian from getting lost in the darkness of introspection or in diffuse religiosity.'[24]

---

24. Martinez, *Praying with the Grain*, 162. *Praying with the Grain* includes a thorough reflection on the therapeutic effects of prayer and Christian meditation, as well as an analysis of Christian prayer in comparison to Eastern meditations and 'the healthy practice of Christian meditation.'

Therefore, if we want to imitate Jesus in this vital area of ministry, we must learn not only from his doing but also from his stopping. We need to set aside specific times to pause and 'be still' before God.

'Feed My Lambs': The Three Steps of Jesus' Restoration

'Jesus said to Simon Peter, "Simon son of John, do you love me more than these? . . . Feed my lambs. . . . Take care of my sheep."' (John 21:15–16)

Spiritual renewal that comes from fellowship with God is paramount, finally, because it is required of us if we are to feed Christ's flock. We cannot nourish others if our needs have not been met first. I have chosen the story of Peter's restoration because it is a masterpiece of renewal. When we feel that we are failures, like useless broken jars, we need to be restored and nourished again.

The way Jesus restored Peter (John 21:15–18) set up a remarkable model of restoration that goes beyond forgiveness after a moral fall. There was indeed forgiveness at this memorable encounter because Peter needed it, but there was also an intensive lesson on renewal. We make a mistake when we limit the idea of restoration to the process of recovery after sin. Restoration—meeting our needs—should come before sin, not after it!

The Master renewed Peter thoroughly by equipping him with three tools that are a requirement for any Christian worker:

1. Renewal of the love for Christ: A fresh motivation

Jesus starts this intensive lesson with a very personal question: 'Peter, do you love me?' The order is deliberate. The first step in restoration is to renew our love for Christ. As Christian leaders, we are not ready to shepherd the sheep before loving the Prince of pastors. The driving force that moves us—our motivation—springs from our love for Christ.

The problem in the church in Ephesus is a permanent reminder for us not to fall into the same error: 'Yet I hold this against you: You have forsaken the love you had at first' (Revelation 2:4). They had done many things well and the angel praises them for 'your deeds, your hard work and your perseverance' (v. 2), but they were found lacking in the essential: their love for Christ.

The loss of the 'love you had at first' is not so much a cooling of feelings as a change in motivation. When Christ ceases to be our central motivation, our ministry loses freshness and we become progressively weakened. Our life may be filled with laudable spiritual activities, as was the case of the church at Ephesus, but the plain fact is that we no longer have our eyes fixed on 'the pioneer and perfecter of faith' (Hebrews 12:2). This is why a constant renovation of the 'first love' becomes a hallmark of our renewal.

Now, what kind of love are we talking about? Jesus' question to Peter gives us the clue: 'Do you love me?' He uses the word *agape* for his first two questions and the term *filio*, the love of a friend, for the third. This helps us grasp the kind of love Jesus refers to. It isn't a question of sentimentality—a simple 'falling in love' with Christ—which, as with all feelings, is subject to fluctuations. *Agape* love is not something spontaneous or natural, but rather a choice that requires effort; it is not an emotion but a decision. Friendship, for its part, is made manifest in loyalty and unwavering faithfulness. Peter had to learn this quality of love for Jesus as a requisite for a fruitful ministry.

It is not easy to love someone you have not seen, as Peter himself hints in his epistle (notice this emphasis in 1 Peter 1:8). In my own experience I find it helpful to picture scenes from the life of Jesus or verses which stimulate gratitude and love in my heart. In this respect, one of my favourite texts is Hebrews 12:2–3, a brief but marvellous portrait of Jesus' life and sacrifice. It is no accident that this passage concludes, 'so that you will not grow weary and lose heart.'

Indeed, when we recall the sacrifice of Christ, we feel overwhelmed and motivated (moved to action). This was the experience of Count von Zinzendorf (1700–1760), who was profoundly impressed by contemplating a painting of the crucifixion with the following inscription: 'I have done this for you. What will you do for me?' This experience was the starting point of the revival movement known as the Moravian Brethren. How right Paul was in saying: 'Christ's love compels us' (2 Corinthians 5:14).

2. Renewal of love for the people of Christ: A genuine compassion

Jesus continues his dialogue with Peter in a fascinating way from a pastoral perspective. After the apostle's response to his initial question, Jesus exhorts him, 'Feed my lambs.' The link between the two sentences is admirable. The natural consequence of the restoration of love for Christ is the renovation of love for Christ's flock. Love for the shepherd clearly entails love for the shepherd's sheep.

When Christ renews motivation, he also renews our compassion for his people. This renewed mercy enables us to serve and love them just as Christ loved his church despite its stains and blemishes. Genuine compassion for and commitment to the people of God is the result of our love for God.

3. Renewal of the calling: A reaffirmed vocation

It is not surprising that Jesus closes his encounter with Peter with just one sentence: 'Follow me' (v. 19). No doubt this firm exhortation sounded as an echo of the first 'follow me' three years earlier. A renewal of the initial calling was necessary at this stage. Once the Master was sure of Peter's love, he gave him a clear commission—'feed my lambs'—and finally, reaffirmed his calling—'follow me.' It is a logical order: our vocation in Christian ministry is nourished by a fresh motivation and a clear commission. Many crises in ministry arise when one or two of these steps fail.

'Take care of yourself' (see 1 Timothy 4:16). If we want to survive and thrive in Christian ministry, the healthiest renewal comes from being still before God and listening to his 'gentle whisper.' Only God can meet our God-shaped needs. The essence of rest lies in resting in God.

Epilogue

'Nevertheless, I will bring health and healing.
. . . I will heal my people and will let them
enjoy abundant peace and security.'

Jeremiah 33:6

One of the most fascinating discoveries I
have made in my practice as a Christian medical
doctor over the years is the close relationship between God's commandments and abundant life. It
is amazing to see how God's truth is a source of
health and peace. In the Bible the three concepts go
together like the legs of a tripod. Health and peace
are inseparable from Truth. Notice these meaningful words: 'I have set before you life and death,
blessings and curses. Now choose life. . . . For the
LORD is your life' (Deuteronomy 30:19–20).

Similarly Jesus stated: 'I have come that they
may have life, and have it to the full (abundantly)'
(John 10:10). This is my favourite verse in the Bible
because in a single sentence it encompasses the
essence of the gospel: full life in Christ. The term
abundant here also means superior, better quality.
This abundant or superior life includes and generates the deep rest that Jesus offered: 'Come to me,

all you who are weary and burdened, and I will give you rest' (Matthew 11:28).

This is the simple yet profound secret of personal renewal, because the authentic care of yourself and real wellbeing can never be fully achieved by your own effort (self-help) apart from God's truth and his abundant life in Christ. Through his grace and power your life and ministry 'will be like a well-watered garden, like a spring whose waters never fail' (Isaiah 58:11) for the glory of God, the building up of his people and your own joy.

Appendix

Troubled by Your Past?

The past can be a painful place to visit. Perhaps there are matters in your life which have remained unresolved for years. Perhaps the other people involved have died, so the peace you long for eludes you. All this makes us more vulnerable to weariness and may become a serious hindrance to being at peace and living 'a quiet life.' That is why we thought it advisable to deal, even briefly, with this painful reality. If it is your experience, we trust this final part of the book will minister to you.

Even if it is not your own experience, it is likely that you will minister to others for whom the past remains a constant and accusing present. We encourage you to read this section and to reflect on its application for your ministry.

Be at Peace with Your Biographical Baggage

'*But one thing I do, forgetting what lies behind and straining forward to what lies ahead.*' (Philippians 3:13, RSV)

'How I wish I could go back and change my past.' Did the apostle Paul ever say this? No such sentiment is recorded in his letters, although he had many reasons to regret his past deeply—as a violent persecutor of the church and an accomplice in the death of Stephen, the first Christian martyr. Yet by the end of his life he was able to exclaim, 'I have fought the good fight, I have finished the race, I have kept the faith. Now there is in store for me the crown of righteousness, which the Lord, the righteous Judge, will award to me on that day' (2 Timothy 4:7–8). The apostle could summarize his life joyfully and be at peace with his dark, even bloody past. How we need the same degree of reconciliation with our own life stories!

We all carry baggage in this life, the burden of past circumstances. But this should not cripple us, nor take away the joy of Christ within us. Investing spiritual and psychological energy in trying to shake off the past is often a waste of time and can be harmful because it nourishes frustration and disappointment, ultimately bringing spiritual dryness.

There is certainly a time for cleaning and for healing in our life. While we cannot always get rid of our past burdens and their consequences, we can indeed lighten their weight. The promise of Jesus, 'Come to me, all you who are weary and burdened, and I will give you rest' (Matthew 11:28), includes the weariness of a troubled past. The Lord's purpose is to make the soothing rest of Christ ours.

Our starting point on this sensitive issue must not be what we believe or feel about ourselves, but what God says. Our own emotional perception may not correlate with spiritual reality. God's verdict is what really matters, 'for we are his workmanship, created in Christ Jesus for good works' (Ephesians 2:10, RSV). The Greek word rendered 'workmanship' is the root of the English word 'poem.' In other words, God is writing a poem with your life! Would you dare to say that he is a bad poet in your case? Surely not. His poem is unique and his artistry is fine.

The Argentinean author Jorge L Borges[25] once said in reference to Kafka: 'Kafka's mastery consisted in his ability to transform tragedies into fables.' A fable is a literary composition with useful or moral teaching, so a thought came to my mind: God is like Kafka, but perfect, magnified. How much more is our loving Father able to transform the tragedies and mistakes of our lives into a purpose-filled story!

This is exactly what God did with many of the greatest characters in the Bible. Sometimes their biographies were shadowed by serious occasional sins, as we see in the lives of Jacob, Moses, David, Jonah or Peter. Other times it was a life which had veered off course for years. Yet God used all these jars of clay abundantly. Let us take heart from the fact that Rahab was included in the list of the heroes

25. A leading Spanish-language essayist and short-story writer (1899–1986).

of faith (Hebrews 11:31). A wrong past and a right ministry are compatible in God's purposes.

So it is better to stop struggling against your past and to think differently—biblically—about it. For God uses you *with* your past, however painful or difficult it was, *not in spite of it.*

The Burden of Family Problems: The Example of Joseph

'You intended to harm me, but God intended it for good.' (Genesis 50:20)

One of the most frequent reasons why Christian leaders may feel troubled by their pasts is because of family relationships. In this sense the life of Joseph is an extraordinary example of how a painful past is not an obstacle to a fruitful life. Joseph's baggage was particularly heavy: born into a family full of conflict, he lost his mother in childhood, he was spoiled by his father and his brothers hated him to death. Many wounds, losses and broken family relationships accompanied him during his childhood and youth.

Then he had to experience the bitterness of exile into a foreign land, the turmoil of sexual harassment and the injustice of a long imprisonment in spite of his innocence. He had many reasons to complain and also some reasons to feel guilty. (He was not free of mistakes, especially in the relationship with his brothers.)

Nevertheless, when he reviewed all these past events he had an amazing sense of God's presence and providence. God was not only leading his steps, but using every circumstance in his life to accomplish good purposes. The luminous words in Genesis 50:20 are memorable: 'You intended to harm me, but God intended it for good' (see also 45:5–8). If your life has been difficult so far, you should underline these words in red. God is able to use very sad and bad events for good. This is his master key in writing the poem of our lives.

Now the question is this: How does God put this transformation into practice?

We cannot change our past, but God can change us through his grace. He changes our vision and attitudes. Grace works in us by providing two supernatural resources: *contentment and forgiveness*. They gradually act upon the most disturbing emotions in relation to our past: *anger and guilt*. They clean the toxic effects of anger—resentment, bitterness, hatred—and relieve the oppressive burden of guilt. They cleanse and heal past wounds. They ultimately bring forth peace where there was turmoil, and joy where there was regret.

Contentment: Making an Ally of Our Past

What did Paul mean by being 'content whatever the circumstances' (Philippians 4:11)? The original word implies being above, or not dependent on, circumstances; its emphasis lies in autonomy, in not being bound by past or present events or problems. So the secret to contentment lies in achieving a degree of 'independence' from past painful events, and not being trapped by the memory of them.

Contentment does not imply agreement with our past

We are not called to accept our past in the sense of being *friends* with it. God never demands that we like—or feel good about—painful memories. Paul said, 'Rejoice in the Lord always. I will say it again: Rejoice!' (Philippians 4:4). But to *be joyful* is not the same as *to feel good*. The joy of the Lord is a profound attitude of serenity, trust and hope that gives inner strength (Nehemiah 8:10). God wants his children to be realists. We are called to give thanks to God *in all* situations, but not *for all* situations.

Neither friend nor foe: An ally

Once we are in Christ, we should not view our past as an enemy or as a paralyzing obstacle anymore, but as an ally. An enemy blocks, hinders; an ally helps and favours the capacity to fight. Contentment means coming to a serene conviction that God can use our life not only in spite of our past, but because of it. When we see our past as an ally, trouble gives way to peace. In this manner, all the energy that we previously used in fighting *against* we can now use in fighting *for.*

The Burden of Unrelieved Guilt: 'Why Can't I Forgive Myself?'

'"Come now, let us settle the matter," says the Lord. "Though your sins are like scarlet, they shall be as white as snow; though they are red as crimson, they shall be like wool."' (Isaiah 1:18)

'I know God has forgiven me, but I cannot forgive myself. Guilt continues to trouble me over the years. Why do I feel like this?' I am often asked this question, even by mature Christians. The reason is that any sin and mistake we make in our life requires two therapeutic acts: *cleaning* (through forgiveness) and *healing*. God's forgiveness is the moral tool that makes us acceptable before him again. Healing is the emotional process that makes us acceptable to ourselves. Now, God's forgiveness is immediate as soon as we confess our sin wholeheartedly. But healing requires time, as for any wound.

When you say, 'I cannot forgive myself,' what you really mean is, 'The healing of the wound is not finished yet.' This is why you continue to feel guilty. The persistence of guilty feelings after genuine confession is not a moral or spiritual problem, but an emotional one. God has forgiven you, you are clean before him, but you have not fully forgiven yourself because you are not yet healed. This experience is particularly common in mistakes and sins related to the body. Sexual wounds are very sensitive and may require a long period of healing. In the meantime, remember the blood of Christ has already cleansed you (1 John 1:7).

Again we need to remind ourselves that we are members of a church, a body whose parts are inter-dependent. Sometimes it takes the discernment of an older Christian to help us recognize our emotions and distinguish them during the healing process. There may be a member of your own local church in whom you can confide and from whom you can seek counsel, or a member of another church in your area with whom you can meet from time to time. We mustn't neglect God's vital means of caring for us through others. [26]

A final important clarification: to forgive (ourselves or others) does not mean to forget. Only God can forgive and forget (Isaiah 43:25; Micah 7:18–19). We cannot expect human forgiveness to erase memories; hoping for that may hinder the healing process. Forgiveness does not remove our memories, but it draws the poison from them. When we forgive, the memory of the painful experience is still there but the resentment, hatred or bitterness is gone. While we cannot wipe away our painful memories and difficult life stories, we have the immense privilege to take them to the cross. There the weight of our past is made lighter and the shadow

---

26. I do not cover in detail the wider nature of what it means to belong to a church, but I commend some form of accountability to all leaders. See chapter four, 'The relationship with close friends.'

of our mistakes dissipates completely because in Christ 'the old has gone, the new is here!' (2 Corinthians 5:17).

What a comfort to know that God uses us not only in spite of our past but through it. Our Heavenly Father is a 'specialist' in restoring ruined lives! A troubled past is certainly not an obstacle for him, because 'if God is for us, who [or what] can be against us?' (Romans 8:31). Therefore, since 'justified through faith, we have peace with God through our Lord Jesus Christ' (Romans 5:1), let us also have peace with ourselves, and with our past.

Questions for Study and Reflection

1. 'Make it your ambition to lead a quiet life.' Surprisingly the Bible speaks more about rest than about work. Take time to meditate on why this is so. In which ways are rest and leisure means to honour God and sanctify your life?

2. 'The problem is not working too much, but resting (renewing) too little.' What practical steps can you take to find the right balance in the practice of the *two movements* (output/input; ministry/monastery)? Start praying for one or two small changes to improve this balance.

3. 'Why do we find it so difficult to put this advice into practice?' Are there specific issues that hinder you from taking care of your own garden? How can you address them?

4. 'My mistakes in ministry wearied me.' Consider what in your own life could lead you to the empty pool syndrome. Try to discover your weak points or mistakes. What steps can you take to correct or prevent them?

5. Evaluate the six relationships—sources of renewal—in your own life (family/church/friends/nature/books and, above all, God). Which are you

most satisfied with? What steps can you take to improve the ones that are weaker?

6. 'Many Christian workers are very good at "cooking" for others, but they neglect to "cook" for themselves.' What do you learn from this sentence? Are there any changes to make, or new steps to take, that may guarantee your own spiritual nourishment?

7. Remarkably, rest and renewal—'waters of rest'—appear to be the first provision of the Good Shepherd (see Psalm 23:2), even before guidance or protection. What practical implications can you draw from this divine priority for your life and for your ministry?

Recommended Reading

From the Lausanne Movement

The Lausanne Legacy: Landmarks in Global Mission. Edited by J E M Cameron (Hendrickson Publishers).

The Cape Town Commitment: A Call to Action. A Study Guide for Small Groups. Compiled by Sara Singleton and Matt Ristuccia (Hendrickson Publishers).

The Cape Town Commitment: Study Edition by Rose Dowsett (Hendrickson Publishers).

Ephesians: Studying with the Global Church by Lindsay Olesberg. Six-week study guide for home groups (Hendrickson Publishers).

Creation Care and the Gospel. Edited by Colin Bell and Robert S White (Hendrickson Publishers).

The Glory of the Cross by James Philip (Hendrickson Publishers).

The Grace of Giving: Money and the Gospel by John Stott and Chris Wright (Hendrickson Publishers).

The Reformation: What You Need to Know and Why by Michael Reeves & John Stott (Hendrickson Publishers).

About the Author

Pablo Martinez, a leading Christian psychiatrist based in Barcelona, has served as chairman of InterVarsity Christian Fellowship (GBU) in Spain and of the Spanish Evangelical Alliance. He was professor of pastoral psychology at the Spanish Theological Seminary. Pablo Martinez is current president in Spain of the Ravi Zacharias Foundation for the Dialogue between Faith and Culture.

Dr Martinez's books are widely read around the world in English and in translation. Pablo is married to Marta, also a medical doctor.

For books, articles, lectures and other resources by Dr Pablo Martinez, see 'Christian Thought' (christian-thought.org). This site was founded by his father, Rev Jose M Martinez, a respected theologian and Christian leader in the Spanish-speaking world.

Lausanne Movement

Connecting influencers and ideas for global mission

The Lausanne Movement takes its name from the International Congress on World Evangelization, convened in 1974 in Lausanne, Switzerland, by the US evangelist Billy Graham. His long-time friend John Stott, the UK pastor-theologian, was chief architect of *The Lausanne Covenant*, which issued from this gathering.

Two further global Congresses followed—the second in Manila, Philippines (1989) and the third in Cape Town, South Africa (2010). From the Third Lausanne Congress came *The Cape Town Commitment: A Confession of Faith and a Call to Action*. Its Call to Action was the fruit of a careful process conducted over four years to discern what we believe the Holy Spirit is saying to the global church in our times. In the words of the *Commitment*'s chief architect, Chris Wright, it expresses 'the conviction of a Movement and the voice of a multitude.'

The Lausanne Movement connects evangelical influencers across regions and across generations: in the church, in ministries and in the workplace. Under God, Lausanne events have often acted as a powerful catalyst; as a result, strategic ideas such as Unreached People Groups, the 10/40 Window, and holistic/integral mission have been introduced to missional thinking. Over 30 specialist Issue Networks now focus on the outworking of the priorities outlined in *The Cape Town Commitment*.

The movement makes available online over 40 years of missional content. Sign up to receive *Lausanne Global Analysis* to your inbox. Watch videos from Lausanne's gatherings. On the website you will also find a complete list of titles in the Lausanne Library.

www.lausanne.org